The Making of a Seer:

A personal journey into the spiritual realms

The Making of a Seer

*A personal journey
into the spiritual realms*

by Erica Christopher

@Copyright 2015—*The Making of a Seer: A personal journey into the spiritual realms*, by Erica Christopher

Published by Erica Christopher

All rights reserved. This book is protected by the copyright laws of the United States of America. This book may not be copied or reprinted for commercial gain or profit. The use of short quotations or occasional page copying for personal or group study is permitted and encouraged. Permission will be granted upon request.

Unless otherwise identified, Scripture quotations are taken from the HOLY BIBLE, NEW KING JAMES VERSION @1982 By Thomas Nelson, Inc. Used by permission by Holman. All rights reserved. All emphasis is the author's own.

All scripture marked (NIV) is taken from the Holy Bible, New International Version 10th Anniversary @ 1995 By Zondervan Corporation. All rights reserved. Used by permission.

All Greek meanings are taken from James Strong's *A Concise Dictionary of the Words in the Greek New Testament: With Their Renderings In The Authorized English Version*. 1890 by James Strong, S.T.D., LL.D.; Print. Public Domain.

All Hebrew meanings are taken from James Strong's *A Concise Dictionary of the Words in the Hebrew Bible: With Their Renderings In The Authorized English Version*. Madison, NJ, 1890. Print. Public Domain.

ISBN 978-1-312-95804-3

Cover design and interior layout by Erica Christopher

Photograph of Erica Christopher on front cover taken by ©Twice The Focus Photography

Photography embellishments and interior graphics created by David Joseph of DMJDESIGNER

Acknowledgements and Dedication

      To my mother who taught me at a very early age to look past the natural appearances and see the heart; My grandmother who tirelessly spoke Jesus into my world; my dear husband who loves me graciously; And my precious precious children who are vessels of God's voice every day—Thank you for your love!

      To the Holy Spirit as He is astoundingly incredible and passionately patient with me every day; To God, the giver of the pen (and all gifts), as without Him this book would not have been written; To Jesus Christ for being my salvation (and my friend).

      And, last but definitely not least, to seers everywhere who are on the verge of possessing their promised land yet teetering with uncertainty and unknowns while suffering persecution and doubt—this book is for you! God Sees You!

Endorsements

What you are about to read is a direct quickening from God. It will activate the gift of seer in you, and confirm this amazing call on your life. Erica is extending to you Great Wisdom of "how to flow correctly with the Spirit of God", how to display the kingdom of God, and how to live and breathe the weight of His Glory. The seer gift is a glorious treasure the Father delights Himself in. Any one on any level of leadership should embrace and encourage the gift of seers in their midst. Meeting Erica was a pure delight. As she mentions in her book about discernment, it took me about half a second to perceive her heart and her anointing in her gift. After years of teaching Prophets, Seers and Watchmen, I can assure you Erica has learned the truth from the Holy Spirit.

I say reading this book will save you years in developing your gift and your intimate relationship with God. This book is the beginning of many more to come from Erica. Thank you Erica.

Apostle Dennis Arnold
Revival Central Ministries for All Nations

I believe it is equally important to see with revelation as well as to hear the word of God. The apostle John encountered this in the first chapter of the book of Revelation. He turned around and SAW the voice of God (Revelation 1:12a). Erica Christopher's book *The Making of a Seer* starts with her journey of how God awakened her life through the power of the Holy Spirit. It is full of revelatory teaching on how to hear the voice of God through dreams, visions, and how to overcome through the power of Jesus Christ.

The Kingdom of God is not a matter of talk but of power, and Erica's book will inspire you to fulfill your destiny.

Adam F. Thompson
Co-Author of the bestselling book,
The Divinity Code: The Keys to Decoding Your Dreams and Vision
www.voiceoffireministries.org

Erica takes us on a personal journey - the spiritual realm is real for all of God's children. Her personal encounters in the spiritual realm encourage us all not to be content with just a head knowledge experience, but to encounter the Father and Holy Spirit realm in a personal way because our God is a very personal God.

Kathie Walters
www.kathiewaltersministry.com

Erica writes from her heart with openness and transparency. She does not just write about the wonderful times with God, but also the struggles and more challenging times. I, too, am a SEER. Although my gift operates in different ways, they are similar in some. It is not a formula, but it will help grow a desire and also understanding. I found this book refreshing and encouraging. It is insightful and will be found helpful to all who seek a depth in God that He made us to experience. We all do not have the same gifts, but for those seeking to understand what is going on within their head as they begin to experience the Spiritual world, this book will be valuable. This is her journey, and yet, I found parts of mine. I believe that many people are SEER's and don't even realize it yet. This is a valuable resource to discover another aspect of the mysteries of God and how He continues to walk with us as we learn and grow in the very gifts He gives and uses in us. Well done Erica!

Cheryl Stasinowsky,
Author and Speaker (and SEER)
www.hishiddentreasure.blogspot.com

I was overwhelmed when I read, *The Making of a Seer*. I have heard many testimonies of people operating in the seer realm but the anointing upon this book will actually bring an "awakening" to the spiritual eyes of the reader and open the door for their own encounters with God. The fruit of this book is not just a compilation of stories but the tangible presence of God you experience as you read the pages of this book. Our God is an encountering

God and this is the book of the hour to raise up a generation of seers.

Mike Rogers, Senior Pastor
The Church at New Bern
New Bern, North Carolina
www.newbernchurch.org

    As a watchman and pastor, I was very pleased when Erica told me about her new book, "The Making of a Seer".

    This ministry and the things she shares in this excellent and challenging book, are so true and applicable for the church today, no matter what part of the world we may live in.

    Knowing Erica for approximately 2 years through social networking, I can honestly say she is very sincere and puts the Lord first in her life. The contents of this book are very encouraging and one can certainly appreciate the things she shares, and her experiences.

    Believe me, things to do with the spiritual realm are very real and even more so if you are called as Erica is, or anyone with a watchman or a seer ministry. It is just as real here in the UK, as I am sure what she writes in this book that have happened are. Hearing Gods voice through dreams and visions is inspiring and very real.

Well done Erica!

Keith Ogden
Pastor, Watchman and Owner of
Timely Bridges Books UK

For many years I have read books written by people who have the ability to see into the spiritual realm. While it is insightful to read about the experiences of others, it becomes quite another thing to see and experience it for yourself. *The Making of a Seer* takes one beyond what all other books have done – it carves out a fresh awakening that "we too" have the ability to see God's unseen world just as Elisha's servant did (2 Kings 6:17). Erica powerfully reinforces God's heart that the discerning of spirits is not only needed in today's church, but is absolutely essential for the times so quickly approaching.

I stand in awe of Erica's honesty, determination, and courage as she opens her heart to unveil before the world the secret things of Heaven.

Kat Beights, Founder and President,
Daybreak International Ministries, Inc.
www.daybreakint.org

Erica is a precious woman of God I have fellowshipped with for the last few years. She is both a seer and a scribe, faithfully recording what she sees and hears. In The Making of a Seer, you will get a first-hand account of her spiritual journey -- one that is based on the heart-to-heart and face-to-face intimacy she enjoys with the Father. Erica's writing is relatable and down-to-earth, just as she is. This is not a formulaic teaching on how to become a seer, but an honest, heartfelt account of how she was molded and shaped not only to see the beauty of God and the host of angels, but to discern more sharply the works of the enemy. This book you hold in your hands contains the precious substance of eternity wrapped up in the humble testimony of this beautiful friend of God.

Sandra L. Martin,
Prophetic Artist & Founder,
Creative Currents
www.creativecurrents.net

As I began to read The Making of a Seer, one word repeatedly came to mind: insightful. Erica takes the reader through her journey of discovering a closer walk with God and what an amazing walk it is. I have known Erica for several years, and she lives the life she portrays in her book. I marvel at her hunger, education and grasp of the spiritual realm. Though we live in the same county in Mississippi, one might re-phrase Nathanael's asking, "Can there any good thing come out of Nazareth? Philip saith unto him, Come and see." (John 1:46) I, also, say "come and see" by reading Erica's book. She is blessed by God with the fivefold ministry gift of prophesy. I am blessed by her sharing of her journey, and I know she will bless others by not only this book but other books sure to come.

Sandra J. Grych,
Communications Instructor, Mississippi

I have just finished reading The Making of a Seer. I want to thank my friend Erica for "answering the call" to equip the saints and for not shrinking back in fear or doubt but boldly trusting in "The One Who Sees" and stepping into her calling! Seated perfectly next to her King, looking and watching. We need your gift! We need the Seers to equip and empower us (to thwart the plan of the enemy) as we go forth "In Christ" to proclaim the good news and set the captives set free—to walk in their calling!

Arise body of Christ and be and do all He has called you to. Read and devour as I have, present your eyes to Him. Become a Seer...

Maureen Rauscher
Chattanooga, Tennessee

I sat down and could not stop reading this book, The Making of a Seer. The Holy Spirit was intense and I felt my Spirit hunger for more—more of the Lord! I am changed, no longer the same. The spirit of fear has lost its hold on me! Praise God!! Thank you my, Erica, for allowing Him to write your story!

Melody Guy
Mississippi

The Making of a Seer is a gift from God. It is the most encouraging and inspiring book that explains the different aspects of the gift of discerning of spirits, that I have ever read. As a seer myself I needed a book like this years ago to help me to understand that I was not crazy! I read everything I could get my hands on but didn't get understanding like she has so beautifully tells—and tells all. Her story reveals understanding of the gift of discerning spirits from which the Seer gift is spoke of in the Old Testament.

Her story is an adventure that shows how our Abba Father tenderly watched and waited as she opened the beautiful gift layer by layer. And as she sought more of this gift He poured more of Himself in with more wisdom and revelation of who she was and who He is. If you are looking for a book to help you grow in your gift of discerning spirits this is a must read. This is not a how to, but rather wisdom on how wonderful our Father is as He waits and watches us grow with His unfailing Love.

Susan Riggs
New Bern, NC

Contents

The Making of a Seer: A personal journey into the spiritual realms

- Endorsements
- The Pen
- The Key of Faith
- Preface
- Introduction

Section One: How it all started...

- Setting the Stage
- The Awakening
- My Pentecost

Section Two: Revealing the Spiritual Realms

- Experiencing Visions
- Becoming a Dreamer
- Learning to Discern
- Discerning the Message
  - A Warning About Discerning
- Seeing Demons
  - The Last Enemy To Be Destroyed
- Seeing Spiritual Things
  - A Word About Rebellion
- Seeing Angels
  - A Word of Caution

- Looking into the Spirit
- Receiving Beforehand

Section Three: Hearing in The Spirit

- Hearing Angels
- Hearing Demons
- Hearing The Spirit of a Man
- Hearing The Thoughts and Intents of the Heart

Section Four: The Fight

- The Battle with Fear
- Pondering The Return
- Blessed Vengeance

Contact Information

Endnotes

The Pen

Even though this book has been burning in my heart for many years now every attempt to write it has failed.

Finally, one day I said to the Lord, "I will write whatever you want me to, but I cannot do it on my own and, Father, I won't do it without a pen. I have read books by authors you've given pens to, and as a result, their books are powerfully moving and life changing. Father, I know that you are no respecter of persons, and what you do for them, you can do for me. So, in light of that, I will wait for my pen."

In September 2014 I was attending the last weekend of the School of the Prophets in Chattanooga, Tennessee, when Prophetess Jan Porubsky, President of Children's Hope International, Inc. asked me to join her at the front of the sanctuary. Not knowing anything of my desire to write or of my asking the Lord for a pen, she took my hand and prophesied the following over me (this prophecy was quite lengthy; therefore, I have shortened it to include only that which pertains to writing):

> Erica, I just want to speak a word over you, precious. Daddy, I just thank you for Erica.

The Lord said that David said my tongue is the pen of a ready writer. He says that He is preparing your hand. And when I held your hand over there, I felt a burning sensation and I feel it now. It's over your right knuckle. I said, "Daddy, what is it?"

He said, "That's the pen. That's a pen I have placed in her hand. So that pen I feel is on fire because it's not your pen; it's His pen. And He's gonna give you the words that you'll pen. He's gonna give you the words.

He says your mouth is the pen of a ready writer. You're gonna write fluently. And He's gonna give you books, more than one. And in those books, you're gonna be able to write. You're gonna be able to encourage others. And you're gonna be able to strengthen others. And you're gonna be able to guide others. And you're gonna be able to teach others.

I just thank you, Father, for what you're doing for Erica, and I give you all the praise, glory, and honor, for it's in Christ's name we pray. Amen. Amen. Amen. Amen. Thank you, Papa. Thank you, Papa.

This book is the first product of that pen. I pray it is powerfully moving and life changing to everyone who reads it in Jesus' name. Amen!

The Key of Faith

Many years ago, early in my walk with the Lord, I asked Him one day what I needed to do to grow in wisdom and knowledge of who He is. Suddenly I saw before me, in the Spirit, a key, and on that key was the word "faith." I reached out with my hand in the natural as if I were reaching for some object. As I did, I saw a door appear before me.

On that door was the word "faith." I took the key and placed it in the doorknob and turned the handle to open the door. I was astonished at what I saw. Inside the door of faith was the entire universe. I saw the earth, the stars, and all the heavens. Everything seen and unseen was located within this door of faith. Hebrews 11:3 says: "Through faith we understand that the worlds were framed by the word of God, so that things which are seen were not made of things which do appear."

As I am standing inside the door of faith, there is yet another key. On this key, however, is the word "doubt." I reached out and took the key. I had to walk out the door of faith to get to the door of doubt, for doubt cannot exist inside faith. As I did this, I saw the door to doubt close. I took the key, locked the door, and then tossed the key away.

As I am writing this, I am seeing yet another key, and this key has the word "fear." Hmm, fear? I am reminded of what Isaiah 33:6 says about the fear of the Lord being a key: "He will be the sure foundation for your times, a rich store of salvation and wisdom and knowledge; the fear of the Lord is the key to this treasure." (NIV)

There are so many treasures awaiting all of God's children; let's get started and reveal some of those treasures.

Preface

In the age of absolute fascination with the spiritual world, many are being pulled deep into the occult. Our society is completely bombarded by vampires, witchcraft, voodoo, and every kind of new age religion. Many are seeking to have spiritual experiences without first seeking the Kingdom of God, but rather simply a "higher power". To access the spiritual realm, many turn to psychics, sorcerers, clairvoyants, mediums, or witchdoctors—Satan! If these people only knew the power they hold in Jesus Christ, they would never SETTLE for a power that is less than who He is.

I had an interesting encounter with my daughter about an hour after I wrote the previous paragraph. We were in the car on our way to her school when she said to me, "Momma, how many dollar bills make a quarter?"

I said, "Well, dollar bills cannot make quarters but quarters can make dollars."

She said, "I don't understand. What do you mean?"

I said, "Well it takes four quarters to make a dollar, but a dollar bill can't be less than a dollar bill."

As I said those words, immediately I heard the Lord say, "I cannot make someone less than who I AM."

You see, God has made available to us all the power He has through His Son, Jesus Christ. Through Him we become more than we are. Through Him we become greater because He cannot make us less than who He is.

The truth is we are spiritual beings and we are drawn to that which is spiritual; however, in the words of Hosea 4:6, "My people are destroyed by a lack of knowledge." God is raising up a generation of Seers. The enemy knows this and is eagerly coming to them as a counterfeit spirit very early. Unfortunately, he is able to do this quite easily because there is a lack of understanding and instruction regarding supernatural experiences within the body of Christ—and the enemy has been able to capitalize on it.

What I find interesting is that the world embraces supernatural abilities, abilities that God created to edify, encourage, and empower His body—the church. The problem is the world is hungry for "more" while the church is happy with "less."

Clairvoyants and mediums are all Seer prophets who are misled or misguided. They are counterfeit workings of the genuine Seer gift. While God is the Spirit behind the Seer, Satan is the spirit behind clairvoyants and mediums. The mere fact that the world desires to dive head first into the supernatural realm of the counterfeit spirit should open the eyes of the church to examine why. The mere existence of this fascination should cause the church to realize it has a blind spot regarding the workings of God. Red flags should be going up and sirens should be blasting inside every Christian's head because Satan has no original power on his own; he can only counterfeit the original.

Introduction

Beloved Reader,

     As I waited for the Lord to tell me how best to introduce you to this book, my heart was suddenly touched and I heard "El Roi, For I Am the God who sees."

     A reverential hush fell over my entire being as I sat completely absent of all words. I felt a stirring deep down inside and I began to understand that this is a very important matter to God. As I sat in this spiritually impregnated atmosphere, I heard these words from 1 Corinthians 2:9-12:

> Eye has not seen, nor ear has heard, nor has it entered into the heart of man the things which God has prepared for those who love Him. But God has revealed them to us through His Spirit. For the spirit searches all things, yes, the deep things of God. For what man knows the things of a man except the spirit of the man which is in him? Even so, no one knows the things of God except the Spirit of God. Now we have received not the spirit of the world, but the Spirit who is from God, that we might know the things that have been freely given to us by God.

By many accounts, the modern-day church has expelled the workings of the Holy Spirit, thus removing the inherited rights of the children of God to know Him and all He has freely given.

When the Holy Spirit is not allowed to work, we are left to understand Scriptures by mere logic and reason. Without the Holy Spirit, however, it is impossible to understand the ways of God let alone the depth of His words and thoughts regarding our lives. For 1 Corinthians 2:14 says, "But the natural man does not receive the things of the Spirit of God, for they are foolishness to him; nor can he know them, because they are spiritually discerned."

The church has done an amazing job at rote knowledge. Psalms 119:9-11 says, "How can a young man cleanse his way? By taking heed according to Your word. With my whole heart I have sought You; Oh Let me not wander from Your commandments! Your word I have hidden in my heart, that I might not sin against You." The more scripture we have embedded within us, hidden within our hearts, the more the Lord can pull out of us in time of need. It is indeed a great thing to be able to quote scripture; however, without incorporating spiritual or supernatural experiences, we will never be able to experience the fullness that God has impregnated within His Word, much less in our lives. For the fullness of these things are spiritual and not obtained through leaning on our own understandings. They require eyes to see, ears to hear, and a heart that understands, and all that requires the Holy Spirit. In fact, scripture tells us in Zechariah 4:6, "Not by might, nor by power, but by *My Spirit* says the Lord of hosts."

The coming of the Holy Spirit on the day of Pentecost marked a new day for the church, a new era when the Lord was no longer a far-off God only reached through sacrifices and high priests, but a God who came to dwell within us, empowering us to know Him in His fullness. For God is Spirit and to know Him is to know the world of the Spirit and to experience supernaturally all He has for us.

The Seer Gift:

1 Corinthians 12:5-11 says:

There are diversities of gifts, but the same Spirit. There are differences of ministries, but the same Lord. And there are diversities of activities, but it is the same God who works all in all. But the manifestation of the Spirit is given to each one for the profit of all: for to one is given the word of wisdom through the Spirit, to another the word of knowledge through the same Spirit, to another faith by the same Spirit, to another gifts of healings by the same Spirit, to another the working of miracles, to another prophecy, to another discerning of spirits, to another different kinds of tongues, to another the interpretation of tongues. But one and the same Spirit works all these things, distributing to each one individually as He wills.

The spiritual gift of the Seer works within the gift of discerning of spirits. Seers are the eyes of the body of Christ. Jesus empowered this amazing gift to many within His body to testify concerning His world—the spiritual world. For within the spiritual world lie treasures untold and an eternity chocked full of life everlasting. It is a world of beauty and wonder where the imaginational aspect of the Heart of God is alive and active, where life abounds and love is alive. It is a place of reality beyond natural reasoning. It is a place where words come to life and accomplish destinies. It is a world where battles are fought, and the fight for your destiny is a constantly raging war. It is a place where God desires for you to live, where you can know Him in the breadth, length, and height of His fullness—His love.

In Ephesians 4:11 Paul says, "And He Himself gave some to be apostles, some prophets, some evangelists, and some pastors and teachers, for the equipping of the saints for the work of ministry for the edifying of the body of Christ." Seers are prophets and the Bible uses two words in regards to seers—ra'ah and chozeh.

Chozeh is a Hebrew word that means "a beholder in a vision," "a prophet," "see," "stargazer." This word can be found in 1 Chronicles 29:29, "Now the acts of King David, first and last, indeed they are written in the book of Samuel the seer, in the book of Nathan the prophet, and in the book of Gad the seer." And in 2 Samuel 24:22, "Now when David arose in the morning, the word of the Lord came to the prophet Gad, David's seer, saying," just to name a couple.

Ra'ah is a Hebrew word that means to see, behold, gaze, discern, visions. This word can be found in 1 Samuel 9:9, "(Formerly in Israel, when a man went to inquire of God, he spoke thus: 'Come, let us go to the seer'; for he who is now called a prophet was formerly called a seer.)" And in 1 Samuel 9:19, "Samuel answered Saul and said, "I am the seer. Go up before me to the high place, for you shall eat with me today; and tomorrow I will let you go and will tell you all that is in your heart." to name a couple.

Seers are part of the fivefold ministry and are God's gift to His church, helping to empower, to equip, and to encourage all saints. They bridge the gap between the seen and unseen realms. They bring the visionary part of the Spirit to the body of Christ and reveal the eyes of God. For through His Seers, God makes known that He is a God who sees us. It is very important to God that you understand HE SEES YOU and He wants you to see HIM.

Life:

At times life seems an aimless compilation of calendar days—where days turn into weeks, weeks turn into months, months turn into years, and before we know it, we're at the end of a season in our lives. Then we ask the infamous questions that seem to flow through our minds as the time on the calendar rewinds: "Where did the time go?" "What did I really accomplish?" "Was all this a waste?" Suddenly the big screen in our minds replays specific events of the life now gone, and we remember battles won or lost in great detail.

It seems that only by examining the past do we understand our future. It is only when we ponder the preparation that we can understand the success. And it seems that only when we understand the success are we encouraged to forge forward to possess the land of our time.

When Moses accumulated all Israel on the banks of the Jordan, he reminded them of their journey during a particular season of their lives, a season where at one time they had asked Moses what their purpose was. At one point they all wanted to throw their hands up and return to the place of their captivity because for some reason it sounded better to them. Moses, remembering the summation of the last forty years, however, reminded them of the great trials their eyes had seen, and the great signs and great wonders needed to deliver them. He reminded them of the fact that even though they'd wandered for 40 years, they had not worn out their clothes nor their shoes. He reminded them of the battles won and territories gained.

And now they stood on the banks of the Jordan in the presence of the One who guided them through it all. On the verge of absolute possession, Moses spoke words of empowerment to the generation that would possess the Promised Land in Deuteronomy 29:10-13:

> All of you stand today before the Lord your God: your leaders and your tribes and your elders and your officers, all the men of Israel, your little ones and your wives—also the stranger who is in your camp, from the one who cuts your wood to the one who draws your water—that you may enter into covenant with the Lord your God, and into His oath, which the Lord your God makes with you today, that He may establish you today as a people for Himself, and that He may be God to you, just as He has spoken to you, and just as He has sworn to your fathers, to Abraham, Isaac, and Jacob.

So often I used to think of myself as just another face in the crowd—nothing in particular, nothing set apart, nothing unique. God doesn't see me that way at all, however, and He doesn't see you that way either. When you come face to face with El Roi—the God who sees—you begin to understand that the eye of God is the eye that sees every detail at once. He sees each member of His creation in the beauty from which He formed it. He calls you by name and knows the number of your days and the hairs on your head. He is specific and personal to each and every one in the purpose for which He created us so that He may be a God to us.

God is standing before you on this day, in the midst of your circumstance, and He's saying, "I am the God who sees YOU. And the spiritual magnitude that I created within your life is enormous, regardless of how small you see your role or how great you see your trials." You may be the one who cuts the wood or draws the water, yet you may also be the one God has ordained to lead a nation. He created you as an individual to have an effect on those around you and to possess the land of your time.

In this book I will share with you the very intimate moment when I met El Roi, the God who sees me and how that encounter changed my life. I will share with you specific examples of how God systematically introduced me to the spiritual realm, how He uses the one He names as Seer, how He is personable to the one being seen, and how through this gift I am forging forward to possess the land of my time.

I want to be careful to point out that although this is my own journey, this gift is not about me. No gift or calling is about the one who bears the weight of it. It is about the amazing love the Father has for His children and His burning desire to cause them to know Him. It's about God wanting to equip, encourage, and edify His people to walk in freedom to possess the land of their time.

This is my fifteenth year of seeing in the spirit, and through the years I have come to know a God who utterly and compassionately LOVES His people. He sees every trial, every temptation, every snare, every tear, every sacrifice, every obedient act—my dear friends, HE SEES YOU!

I pray that as you read through my testimony, you will fall head over heels in love with Jesus and His unseen realms as He has fallen head over heels in love with you. I pray that if you are challenged by the stories I share in this book that you spend some time in conversation with God—that you allow Him to stretch you to new heights and greater distances; that you allow Him to take you out of your comfort zone and into a new territory; that you allow Him to remove all blinders, all mindsets, all religious ideas; that you allow Him to reveal the unseen and the undiscovered to you—His hidden treasures. I pray that you are encouraged by my journey to forge forward to possess all the possibilities He has for your life, to fight to be an overcomer for "Eye has not seen, nor ear heard, Nor have entered into the heart of man the things which God has prepared for those who love Him" (1 Corinthians 2:9).

Section One

How it all started...

Setting the Stage

"Delight yourself also in the Lord, And He shall give you the desires of your heart." (Psalm 37:4)

My very first memory of hearing the name "Jesus" came from the lips of my precious grandmother when I was about four years old. I can still see her blue eyes as she talked about the Father, the Son, and the Holy Spirit as she read to me from the pages of her well-worn Bible.

My grandmother said to me quite emphatically when I was five years old, "Erica, never renounce the name of Jesus—never! No matter what happens, never renounce His name!" As she was saying this to me, I saw a time in the future when evil men would come out of the wilderness and seek to kill those who would not renounce the name of Jesus. At the time, I had no understanding of what I was seeing, so I tucked it away. That vision is just as vivid today as it was so many years ago.

Most of my childhood memories are infiltrated with some kind of church event. My family was present and accounted for every Sunday morning, every Sunday night, and every Wednesday night. When I was eight years old, I walked the aisle of a little ole country church and accepted Jesus as my Lord and Savior.

Life carried on and I drifted away from the Lord. A few years, a wedding, and two kids later, when I was 25 I felt the Holy Spirit drawing me intensely to return to the Lord. So my husband and I joined the local First Baptist Church, and shortly thereafter, I started attending one of the church's women's Bible studies.

Week after week I met with other stay-at-home moms who were insatiably hungry for Jesus. As we worked our way through one Bible study after another, I began to grow in the Lord once again. This time, however, I didn't just grow in the knowledge of Him; I fell in love with Him, and I couldn't seem to get enough of Him. With each study, my love for Jesus intensified and I was utterly and compassionately delighted in learning all I could about Him.

In the summer of 1999, our women's group began a study called *To Live is Christ* by Beth Moore, which is a study of the life of Paul. Up until this point, all our studies were solely about building a relationship with Jesus, so when this study came across the table for discussion, I wholeheartedly, hands-down voted no. I didn't have anything against Paul, but we had built up a momentum of growing in Jesus and I didn't want to hinder that flow by shifting gears. I had very little interest in learning about someone else's life—my heart was to *know* more about Jesus. I was overruled, however, and we started our venture into Paul's life. Little did I know that the Lord had something very special in store for me during this study, and my knowledge of Him was about to catapult.

The Awakening

Then she called the name of the Lord who spoke to her, You-Are-the-God-Who-Sees; (Genesis 16:13)

It was early in the morning and my house was very still and quiet when I got up. I grabbed my Bible and workbook and headed off to my quiet place. We were about midway through the study, and on this particular day, our lesson was about Paul's conversion on the road to Damascus.

As I read through the conversion, I sat absolutely speechless! Not that the conversion account was anything new to me; I had read this story many times throughout my life. On this particular morning, however, Paul's conversion felt so different and I was overwhelmed at God's choice of vessels. No longer was I merely reading the words off the page. It felt as though I was hovering over center stage as Saul entered from stage right and then collided with the voice of the Lord in a blinding flash. I could all but feel the sandy road beneath my feet and breathe in the dry air.

As time seemed to freeze, I remember so clearly saying to the Lord, "Lord, my goodness! You chose this guy? He persecuted Your people and now You're choosing him? By his own words, he was "circumcised the eighth day, of the stock of Israel, of the tribe of Benjamin, a Hebrew of the Hebrews; concerning the law, a Pharisee; concerning zeal, persecuting the church; concerning the righteousness which is in the law, blameless." Even though my heart was captivated, my carnal mind couldn't imagine what God was thinking when He chose Paul. So I began thinking forward through the timeline of Paul's life and remembered all the incredible things he accomplished for the kingdom of God—I was in awe over where God had taken Saul from to where He took Paul to—from executioner to apostle. Only God could do something like that. Then I began examining my own life and said, "Well, Lord, I have never persecuted your people. So what could you do with me?"

Within seconds, a booming stillness filled the room, a stillness that seemed so loud it made my ears vibrate. It was as though my words opened a heavenly portal and suddenly out of the silence I heard the audible words, *"I AM the God of Paul."* Now I am not sure how to describe that moment, as everything within me was apprehended. How do you describe a moment when God the creator, the sustainer of all life speaks to you and you can hear His words with your own ears?

Something was happening to me, even though I had no grid for understanding it. Suddenly, however, I began to comprehend a God who was not just a God of biblical times or yester year, but a God who was a God of right now. In those few seconds, God became a living being to me and everything became different. It was the most overwhelming moment of my life. It was a time when I came face to face with the Creator of the universe and He introduced Himself to me saying, "I AM the God of Paul." It was a time when I realized the Great I AM was seeing me. Now it was I who was colliding with the voice of the Lord on center stage, yet it didn't feel like a blinding flash. It felt more like time suddenly stood still.

Suddenly every Bible story I had ever been taught became a possibility for my own life. I was immersed in the tangible presence of the living God, and in one moment of time, my world, as I knew it, was forever changed.

A that point, every religious box of Him ever presented to me seemed too small. I realized He was bigger than any doctrine or religion and He spanned not only biblical times, but all of time. The God of "way back then" is talking to me and I can hear Him with my own ears today. The very voice that spoke to Saul on that dirt road to Damascus is speaking to me and I am known by Him. I am seen by Him. I was utterly and completely changed!

Somehow I seemed to make it out of my quiet place that morning, though I fumbled through the myriad of my daily activities. I could think of nothing other than the reality of a God who is living and interactive. As the truth of that early morning moment began to sink in, my mind started exploring the possibilities of a completely different realm. I remembered John 4:24, which says, "God is Spirit, and those who worship Him must worship in spirit and truth." *God is Spirit...must worship in spirit,* I thought. *What does this mean? If God is Spirit and we are to worship Him in spirit, then there has to be a spiritual place...an entirely differently realm—a realm that is beyond this natural world; a realm where the Spirit of the living God resides; a realm that truly never dies and has always lived; a realm that sees me and knows me right here and right now, this very second; a realm that can interact with me*—I was astonished. A spiritual realm—I spent my whole life in church; how did I miss this?

    I suddenly felt connected to every biblical personality I had ever read about. It was as though I was seeing an invisible thread that had been weaved throughout the generations of all time—the invisible thread—the voice of God. What an amazing hope that began to overtake me as I began to realize that if God still speaks to people this way, then everything He made available to Moses, Joshua, Jeremiah, and Jesus...is available to me. The truth of Malachi 3:6, "For I *am* the Lord, I do not change;" began to take root in my heart and I began to understand that God is truly the God of the living and not the dead. And it is not God who has changed but man's thoughts and expectations of Him. Man has reduced God down to a memory kept alive only through faulty traditions and doctrines as His voice has been silenced in our churches. We elect church leaders to sit as council and elders yet they do not believe in laying on of hands or anointing with oil. How has this happened? On a weekly basis pews are filled with many who stand and sing hymns to a God who lived but is not living and a God who spoke but is not speaking. Where is God's voice in our churches? Where is His Holy Spirit? I was overwhelmed as I began to realize that the Bible is not just a nice collection of stories, but an instructional book of life—for the living.

Over the next few days, I began to flip through the scriptures and noticed times where God introduced Himself to others the same way He did me, with the very words, "I am the God of":

- "And the Lord appeared to him the same night and said, 'I am the God of your father Abraham; do not fear, for I am with you. I will bless you and multiply your descendants for My servant Abraham's sake.'" (Genesis 26:24)
- "'I am the God of Abraham, the God of Isaac, and the God of Jacob'? God is not the God of the dead, but of the living."(Matthew 22:32)
- "But concerning the dead, that they rise, have you not read in the book of Moses, in the burning bush passage, how God spoke to him, saying, 'I am the God of Abraham, the God of Isaac, and the God of Jacob'"? (Mark 12:26)
- "...saying, 'I am the God of your fathers—the God of Abraham, the God of Isaac, and the God of Jacob.' And Moses trembled and dared not look."(Acts 7:32)

When I read those scriptures, I knew I had really heard His voice. This only deepened my newfound burning desire to know more, as suddenly "more" became a vast bottomless vat of knowledge.

My Pentecost

"And suddenly there came a sound from heaven, as of a rushing mighty wind, and it filled the whole house where they were sitting." (Acts 2:2)

A few days after I heard the voice of God, He visited me yet again. This time He came in a whirlwind. I remember laying down one evening to take a nap when suddenly I was no longer in my bed, but in my back yard. I was walking in from the field behind our home, and as I looked around, I saw animals of all kinds walking toward me from the field. As I started walking faster and faster toward the house, a wind started blowing from the North. It was a gentle breeze at first, but with each step I took, the wind became stronger and more robust. By the time I reached out to touch the doorknob, the mighty wind enveloped me and I was no longer standing on my own. It rushed into my mouth and down into my lungs, engulfing every part of me—filling every ounce of my being.

Unexpectedly there was a quietness, a calmness, and a stillness within the mighty wind even though it was still gusting. I heard a soft, gentle voice saying, "Do not silence your speaking." I opened my mouth to try and talk and found I could hardly form words. It felt as though the wind had hold of my voice. I opened my mouth again to form words and just barely a whisper came out. I tried again and again to speak, and with each attempt, my voice got stronger and louder until suddenly I was shouting the words "IN JESUS' NAME!"

Just as fast as the mighty wind came, it was gone, and I found myself back in my room. Even though I felt as if I had gained the attention of my family by shouting, when I opened my eyes everything was just as still as it was before I laid down. I was stunned once more! *What on earth was that all about?* I wondered. *How can this happen? How can I be somewhere else but be here at the same time? How can I be shouting at the top of my lungs, yet no one in the house heard me?* It seemed one question led to another and yet another. What was happening to me? I was in awe once again when on the following day I came across this scripture in Acts 18:9, which says, "Now the Lord spoke to Paul in the night by a vision, "Do not be afraid, but speak, and do not keep silent."

Section Two:
Revealing the Spiritual Realms

Experiencing Visions

"Then He said, 'Hear now My words: If there is a prophet among you, I, the Lord, make Myself known to him in a vision; I speak to him in a dream.'" (Numbers 12:6)

My life felt different now, as if it was written in the pages of the Bible. *What is this book,* I thought, *that it holds the answers to my questions—that it explains this phenomenon I am experiencing?* This instructional book for the living seems to be living itself, as words seem to illuminate upon reading them. It is as though embedded deep within the furrows of verse realms come alive: "The Word of God is living and active"; "The words that I speak to you are spirit, and are life"; "Hear now My words: If there is a prophet

51

among you, I, the Lord, make Myself know to him in a vision; I speak to him in a dream."

Night after night after experiencing the Lord in a whirlwind, as I got into bed and quieted myself before the Lord, I began to see snapshots, pictures in my mind. This was quite startling at first; however, there was also a since of peacefulness as I only experienced seeing these pictures while in a time of worship. Imagine with me, if you will. Close your eyes. What do you see? Nothing but black blank space, right? Now imagine a full-color image complete with the tiniest of details suddenly appearing as if someone had literally just handed you a photograph of something and you were now looking at it. Now let's go a step further and imagine that upon seeing this picture you also have an understanding about it that goes beyond what you're seeing. This is very similar to what you would experience if you were looking at a familiar photograph of your own and while seeing it you're remembering the events that were occurring while the picture was being made. This is God giving you a word of knowledge about that picture He just gave you. It may be a simple word of knowledge and feel more like a knowing; however, it is enough for you to pray and for God to move and meet that need. One of the earliest images I remember, for example, was of a baby who had a broken arm. The baby's face was the image I saw and the fact that it had a broken arm was the knowing or word of knowledge. God was making Himself known as He wanted someone to pray for that broken arm so He could move and answer that prayer.

Most of the images I saw in my early days of visions were much like this. Over time, however, the visions turned into full-color video clips that would play sometimes for hours. I would watch and pray for each image until I fell asleep each night. I had no idea whether I was doing what God wanted me to do, but I remembered watching a healing evangelist on television a time or two and hearing him mention seeing "pictures" of people flashing before his eyes for him to pray for. At the time I had no idea what he was talking about; however, it was making more sense now.

All of this was so new to me. I grew up Southern Baptist and not a part of any apostolic church. In fact, I had never even attended a church that moved in the gifts of the spirit. I had head knowledge of them but that was it, quite honestly I never knew there was anything more. I had a huge learning curve, and it seemed to show no end in sight as after a time, these snapshots began occurring throughout my days, as well. Suddenly a word or an image would flash before my eyes, followed by a person's face. Or I would see a scripture and then see a person's face. The Lord was connecting the image, scripture, or word to the person it applied to. Over time, I learned the purpose of this was for me to pray for the people involved or provide a word of encouragement for them.

One afternoon, for example, I saw the word "turf," appear before me, followed by the face of a dear friend of mine. I sent her a text and told her about the vision I had just seen. She texted me back rather quickly and said, "Would you like to know the story that goes along with that?" Intrigued as I always am, I immediately called her up. She began to share with me that she had a dream the previous night that she parked her car on her brother's neighbor's lawn, which made him a bit angry. That was when I realized the Lord was giving me the interpretation of her dream through my vision—it was a warning that someone would be defending his or her "turf" against my friend.

    The Lord used this method on a daily basis to build my faith and confidence that the messages I was receiving were from Him. This may seem a bit simplistic, a simple picture and then a face, but when God is trying to merge realms with us, we must take baby steps first. We must all crawl before we can run.

Becoming a Dreamer

Then He said, "Hear now My words: If there is a prophet among you, I, the Lord, make Myself known to him in a vision; I speak to him in a dream." (Numbers 12:6)

Simultaneously, as I began having visions, I also began to have dreams that were as real as reality itself. While this was new to me, it also felt familiar because when God spoke to me, He awakened a part of me that had been sleeping and I began to remember dreams I had when I was very young. Now, however, the Lord was beginning to build an understanding with me and connect what I was dreaming to scripture.

The first dream I had after hearing the voice of God was a vivid representation of Joel 2. It was day, yet it was night, and darkness was all around. I saw people gathering, and above in the thick darkness, I watched as the moon turned to blood. Then I woke up and sat straight up in bed, stunned, wondering what on earth that was all about. The next morning while I was reading scripture, I came across Joel 2 and was in awe. *Oh my goodness,* I thought! That was the dream I had, which seemed to be the second half of the vision I had when I was five.

Since that time, my dream life has escalated and it is a rare night when I don't dream. Most of my dreams are directional prophetic happenings of future events regarding my life, my family, my friends, my region, or my country.

It is important to know and then to remember that God often speaks to us in our dreams by way of symbolic speech. Many times the message is very simple; however, we tend to complicate the Lord, even though God is not the complicated one; man is. So in trying to understand what the Lord says to us in dreams, we tend to over think the obvious because we are not thinking symbolically but rather literally.

In prayer one morning the Lord said to me that He would reveal the plans of the enemy to me. Since then it is a rare night when He does not show me some evil plan of the enemy in my dreams. There are even times when I have been taken by the Holy Spirit and an angelic host into the enemy's camp. In these experiences I always feel completely safe and undetected by the demonic kingdom. I am able to hear and see everything that is taking place; however, the demons are not able to see or hear me.

A few years back, for example, I had a dream the Holy Spirit and my angel escorted me into the second heaven. Upon our arrival, I immediately noticed some type of demonic boot camp underway. I saw higher level demons acting as drill sergeants to other demons in formation, performing various types of exercises on a training field. I could hear the grunts and growls and see their ghoulish faces and distorted bodies as they trained. They seemed to be a hodgepodge of recruits. Off to one side I saw busses of new arrivals being unloaded near the training field.

As the Holy Spirit, my angel, and I walked through the demons' camp, we came to a different type of training area. In this area the demons took on a more humanlike appearance in stature and very muscular. Their faces were still highly distorted with pronounced features. This area was more like fencing practice; however, they were not using swords. They were using a flag pole complete with the American Flag and eagle on top. As I stood and watched, I saw demons gouging Americans' eyes out with this weapon, and I heard one of them say, "We will destroy them with their very own freedoms and they will never see it coming."

I was reminded of 2 Corinthians 4:4, which says, "whose minds the god of this age has blinded, who do not believe, lest the light of the gospel of the glory of Christ, who is the image of God, should shine on them." This experience is a great example of how the spiritual realm works and is displayed in our dreams.

On a more personal level regarding evil plans, our home is in Mississippi where the vast majority of U.S. slavery rested, historically. As African slaves were brought over, so were their practices, such as all forms of witchcraft, including black as well as white magic, and voodoo.[i] Much of what I battle in my dreams, therefore, is witchcraft because that is the predominate evil in my region, however, nationally witchcraft is on the rise.

Recently I had a dream that I was laying down and looking up and out through my eyes, as though I was looking through clear water. I saw two dark people standing over me and heard the word "voodoo." I immediately rebuked and broke off the evil curse of voodoo in Jesus' name and woke up. 1 Corinthians 3:16-17 says, "Do you not know that you are the temple of God and that the Spirit of God dwells in you? If anyone defiles the temple of God, God will destroy him. For the temple of God is holy, which temple you are." Those practicing voodoo were attempting to defile this temple. The Holy Spirit who dwells within me alerted me of this and I was able to cancel the curse in Jesus' name.

On a more pleasant note, the Lord also reveals the plans of heaven. Amos 3:7 says, "Surely the Lord God does nothing unless He reveals His secret to His servants the prophets." As I am writing this, the Lord is reminding me of a particular dream where I was visiting a small town. I saw an angel standing on the levee of a huge reservoir with a bulldozer working beside him. The bulldozer was working hard, moving the dirt that held back the water. The angel shouted to me with great excitement, "We have been working all night! The levee is about to break! It shouldn't be long now!" In the next scene, I saw a small town flooded with water at various levels and angels directing cars through the water. The people of the town were very excited.

Now, in the natural, it's not such a great thing if your town gets flooded. In the dreams, however, water represents the Holy Spirit, dirt obviously represents sin or flesh, and cars represent ministry. God was telling me in this dream that the people of the town had been praying and they were about to experience a huge breakthrough that would release the Holy Spirit to move and flow through the entire town. Ministries would flow with new direction and lives would be changed. Praise the LORD!

Dreams are also a way in which we receive spiritual things that aid us in our callings—such as a Discover card. One morning in prayer on July 6, 2014, I was quickened to turn in my Bible to the Gospel of Mark. Not knowing any other specifics I simply started reading at chapter one, verse one. While I was enjoying the read, nothing was really standing out to me but then I came to chapter 9 verses 22-23. These verses were quickened and seemed to suddenly illuminate and hover above the page: "...But if You can do anything, have compassion on us and help us. Jesus said to him, "If you can believe, all things are possible to him who believes."

I was intrigued by this simply because I know the Lord knows I believe. So this quickening had to mean something more. Three days later, on July 9, 2014, the more came. I had a dream where I was handed a Discover card. As I was holding it in my hand I clearly saw the Discover card logo in full color and heard "Discover the Possibilities. Everything is possible. The Game Changer!" Upon awakening and pondering this word from the Lord, I heard, "I AM about to step into some bleak situations and amp up the GAME – I AM about to invoke the 'everything is possible!'" So excited over this word, I shared it with the presbytery team I was on at the time. They in turn took it and ran with it, releasing it over a multitude of prophetic streams. Here is the thing with the Discover card—it is an invitation to experience the game changing anointing of the 'everything is possible' believing power! Believing power allows you the ability to change any situation. Jesus, when approached in Matthew 9:28, asked the blind man, "Do you believe that I am able to do this?" The blind man simply replied "Yes, Lord." According to his faith—his believing power—the blind man experienced the reality of the 'everything is possible.' In one game changing moment he was able to see and a brand new world of possibilities suddenly became available to him. God so desires for us to simply say to Him in every situation we encounter in life, "You, oh Lord, are the Game Changer—I believe You can change this situation." When we use that card—the game changing card—we will discover the endless possibilities of everything being possible.

    Dreams are a very important way that God speaks. It is a time when our minds are shut off from the business of the world and our "thinker" is not thinking. It is a time when the Lord can download very important directional information to us. Consider the importance of the account mentioned in Matthew 1:20-21 when the Lord appeared to Joseph in a dream and announced the forthcoming Son of God:

> But while he thought about these things, behold, an angel of the Lord appeared to him in a dream, saying, "Joseph, son of David, do not be afraid to take to you Mary your wife, for that which is conceived in her is of the Holy Spirit. And she will bring forth a Son, and you shall call His name Jesus, for He will save His people from their sins."

Then later in Matthew 2:12, "Then, being *divinely warned* in a dream that they should not return to Herod, they departed for their own country another way."

Job places the utmost importance on dreams when he says in Job 33:15-18:

> In a dream, in a vision of the night, When deep sleep falls upon men, While slumbering on their beds, Then He opens the ears of men, And seals their instruction. In order to turn man from his deed, And conceal pride from man, He keeps back his soul from the Pit, And his life from perishing by the sword.

Wow! That is a very powerful scripture about dreams—"To save his soul from the Pit and his life from perishing by the sword." Yet dreams are completely discounted by many as aimless wandering of the mind while asleep or better yet a bad reaction to last night's dinner.

I had a dream a couple of years ago that was plainly detailed, not in symbols. It was very direct. At the end of the dream, I heard the words, "Seal it up," and I saw the contents of the dream being folded up as if it were paper and a seal placed at its closure. Then I heard the words, "Your instructions are sealed." Upon waking, I recalled the verse from Job I just quoted. Then I prayed and thanked the Lord for providing me with instructions that will preserve my life. While I couldn't remember any of the dream once I awakened, I remembered the enormity of its contents and I understood from the Lord that this magnitude of information was delivered this way because I would not receive it in any other format. So, in order to accomplish His will, the Lord caused His words to be sealed for my protection.

Over the years, I have learned when the dream is the most direct, the task required is going to be very difficult. That's why the Lord wants to make His instructions to us as clear as possible. On the other hand, when the dream is the most complicated and complex, the task is usually not very hard for us to do.

About 10 years ago, I had a dream where I saw a young married couple arrive at my sister's house. The wife was in labor and about to give birth. In the dream, I saw that the baby would be a boy and the couple was to name the child Ethan. Now that doesn't sound very complicated, does it? Seems pretty straightforward, right? Well, it seems that way because it was. The following day, the Lord provided an encounter and I saw the husband. I shared with him that I had a dream about him and his wife the night before and asked him if he wanted to hear it. Of course he did, so I shared the dream with him. As we stood there, I saw his face drain of all color and he said, "Wow! We haven't told anyone this news yet. We found out a few days ago that we were going to have a boy and we were trying to decide between the names of Ethan and Evan. We have been praying about it."

I said, "Well, there you go. There's your answer. The Lord wants you to name him Ethan."

Ok, here is where it gets difficult. That pregnancy ended in a miscarriage. What an emotionally difficult experience to walk through, one that is always laden with brokenhearted questions. Although this experience was a great surprise to my friends, it was of no great surprise to the Lord. He knew it was going to happen. He knew their hearts and the pain they would feel, so in loving them as He does, He wanted to encourage them by sending a very personal word to encourage them. Remember Numbers 12:6, "Then He said, 'Hear now My words: If there is a prophet among you, I, the Lord, make Myself known to him in a vision; I speak to him in a dream.'"

The young couple ended up becoming pregnant again shortly after this experience and delivered a precious healthy baby boy. They named him Evan, the other name they had chosen. You see, in this dream from the Lord, they were given a *promise* that they would have a baby boy. They were to name the first baby Ethan, which meant the first baby was a boy, as well. By default, the

Lord commissioned the name of their second son, Evan. Essentially the Lord said, "They are to name this baby Ethan because the second baby is going to come along and I want his name to be Evan." Names are very important and carry much of our spiritual identity. Ethan, which means "solid, enduring" was sown as a seed for Evan, which means "God is gracious." Ethan will live forever in heaven, his destiny solid and enduring, and one day he will meet his parents face to face. Until then, the promise of a gracious God will live out his destiny here on earth. What a precious encouragement and act of enduring love from the Lord.

One final word about dreams before moving on. Through the years the Lord has used dreams to confirm to me where I am spiritually in relation to my walk towards Him. Here is what I mean. There are dividing lines that we cross, points of graduation if you will, where we are found faithful in the little and are granted access to more. The dividing line that I am referring to here defines the place where you are no longer living for yourself but have truly laid down your life and have become crucified with Jesus. It is a place of death to self and life in Him. This is beyond salvation. This place is entered only by choosing to be obedient in everything putting aside worldly desires and self-gain. This is the place of intentionally choosing to listen to His voice rather than your own in every decision. It is a place where you are no longer living but it is He who lives through you.

Shortly after I returned to the Lord, I will share more about that later on, I had a dream that takes my breath away even now—years later. In this dream, I suddenly saw before me as if I had been transported back two thousand years to the dry dusty ground at the Praetorium. On bended knee I was face down and could see the ground in great detail that lay before me. I could see sandals in dark brown leather as they crisscrossed up the legs of the Roman soldiers. I could hear the rants and shouts of the angry and hostile crowd. I could feel the warmth of blood oozing down my back and across my brow. I could feel the weight of a wooden beam across my shoulder. With certainty and great difficulty I stood to my feet carrying my cross. Softly the scene faded away and reemerged as I willingly laid down my life. As I took my place I saw not only my feet and hands but also those of Jesus. I watched as the soldiers nailed my feet and prepared to nail my hands. Then softly the dream faded away and I lay wake in my bed.

Luke 9:23-24 says, "Then He said to them all, "If anyone desires to come after Me, let him deny himself, and take up his cross daily, and follow Me. For whoever desires to save his life will lose it, but whoever loses his life for My sake will save it."

Learning to Discern

"And they shall teach My people the difference between the holy and the unholy, and cause them to discern between the unclean and the clean"
(Ezekiel 44:23)

    I was growing more intrigued each day, as each day seemed to be better than the one before. The unveiling layers of the invisible realms suddenly appearing before my eyes caused me to all but jump out of bed each morning. An unexplainable excitement filled my being as the wonder of heaven permeated the atmosphere. And while my nightlife was busy with dreams, and I had become accustomed to visions, my days would soon be filled with seeing unexpected flashes of lights and sparkles around people.

    I remember meeting with the ladies in my Bible study group and being completely distracted by the beautiful array of colors as the lights seemed to dance among us. These were angels and their presence seemed to bring a joy and excitement as the atmosphere felt charged with peace and love.

    Contrary to the peace and love the angels were bringing, I began to notice that certain places felt chaotic, confusing, and unstable. Have you ever stepped on an ant hill and watched as the ants scrabbled furiously in all directions? Well, when I walked into a place that contained demons, that was what the atmosphere felt like.

When discerning the spirits surrounding individuals, the spiritual detection is often expressed through emotions—anger, fear, sadness, happiness. The change is usually dramatic and unmistakable. Sometimes it starts as just a sense of doom and darkness or a sense of peace. Other times it is more specific such as depression, anxiety, aggression, pride, love, rage, hate, or frustration. Demonic spirits reflect their names. So if I am sensing depression around someone, then that is the spirit at work in that person. Once I saw a lady I had not seen in a long while. Upon meeting her, I immediately felt a sense of doom and gloom and suddenly experienced feelings of depression. Looking into the spiritual realm around her, I saw a black hazy cloud resting on her shoulders. She, at first, didn't verbalized any depression. In fact, she was quite cheerful; however, I felt the prodding of the Holy Spirit to minister to her, so I shared with her that even though she seems really happy I sensed that there was something bothering her. She immediately broke down in tears and said, "I am so depressed! I can't shake it. It's like a dark cloud is just following me everywhere I go." I spent some time ministering to her and then upon leaving this lady's side, all the emotions that I felt departed as well. At times I meet someone and become nauseated or may experience a sudden crushing headache, not because of the person, but because of the particular spirit around him or her. This, again, is a physical reaction to a spiritual detection.

I remember once I was standing outside of one of Jay Bartlett's deliverance meetings, as we were on a break, when I suddenly felt the darkest most menacing presence I had ever felt come up behind me. I am not sure what I expected to see when I turned around, but I was a bit shocked to see a small framed five-foot-tall lady. Outwardly she appeared no different than anyone else around her, yet her spiritual appearance was completely different. In the Spirit I saw her as having very pale skin with lacerations on her face. Her eyes were completely black. I was overwhelmed with the feelings of torment and terror this young lady was enduring. My heart broke for her. She did get ministered to during the meeting; however, this type of darkness takes time to exorcise. Please pray for her continued deliverance.

Discerning of Spirits is the gifting in which the entire Seer anointing operates. Found in 1 Corinthians 12:10, the word "discern" in the Greek is *diakrisis,* and it comes from another Greek word, *diakrino*,[ii] which means "to separate thoroughly." Discerning the spirits means thoroughly separating the holy from the unholy—angels from demons. Ezekiel 44:23 says, "And they shall teach My people the difference between the holy and the unholy, and cause them to discern between the unclean and the clean."

When you're discerning angels, you will experience a sense of peace and holiness. Depending on the level of authority the angel is endowed with, you will also experience a sense of reverential fear—a holy fear as the weight and glory of the Lord is felt. This fear is not a tormented fear but rather a fear that allows you to honor the message the angels bring as they come with the holiness and purity of the Father.

The sensations are altogether different when discerning demons. Here, you would feel an absence of peace, holiness, and purity. You will sense a presence incapable of producing a *true* countenance that is reflective of heaven. John warns us in 1 John 4:1-3 to test the spirits because not every spirit is of God and then in 2 Corinthians 11:14 Paul says that Satan himself transforms himself into an angel of light. Demons are deceiving and manipulative just like their master and can present themselves as of the Lord. For this reason, it is vitally important to discern. The only way to learn this supernatural ability is by getting to know God's character and His heart. You must know the scriptures *and* you must know His Spirit.

I was in a meeting with two Seer friends, Kat and Michelle. We had been talking about some things of the Spirit for quite a while when suddenly Kat looked over my shoulder and said, "What is that over there? I see something but can't tell what it is." I turned to look where she was pointing and even though I didn't see anything, I could feel a presence. My other seer friend, Michelle, turned and looked and saw someone crouched against the wall. We asked who he was and Michelle reported that he told her he was sent to follow Christians and that he had a big smile on his face. I immediately discerned this was not a holy spirit, so I asked for a scripture for his assignment. Well, he blurted out John 3:16, which has nothing to do with "following Christians." So I called his bluff and told him he had to leave in Jesus' name. Michelle, who could see him, reported he was no longer smiling. Kat spoke up and told him to confess that Jesus Christ is Lord. Michele started to say something, and as she did, I heard a horrible scream in the Spirit. Michelle verified this by reporting he was now screaming horribly. She looked at me and asked if I could hear it, and I told her I could. As soon as I said that, Michelle reported that he left.

"Sent to follow Christians" he said. Well that was the truth in a twisted kind of way – he was really a spy, an eavesdropper from the enemy camp. A holy spirit would never scream at the command to confess Jesus Christ as Lord. In fact, you would have a harder time getting a holy spirit to stop confessing Jesus Christ is Lord.

Discerning the Message

"I will stand my watch And set myself on the rampart, And watch to see what He will say to me,"
Habakkuk 2:1

When I was still very young in learning to discern the messages the Lord was giving me, He said to me one morning, "I want you to write down all that you are shown." So, I created a journal and called it "Dwelling with the Holy Spirit" with Habakkuk 2:1-3 as my banner.

> I will stand my watch and set myself on the rampart, And watch to see what He will say to me, And what I will answer when I am corrected. Then the Lord answered me and said: "Write the vision And make it plain on tablets, That he may run who reads it. For the vision is yet for an appointed time; But at the end it will speak, and it will not lie. Though it tarries, wait for it; Because it will surely come, It will not tarry.

Conscientiously, I kept a pen and a notepad ready to write as I received. Everything I received, holy and unholy, was meticulously written in my journal. Each time I received a message whether it was spoken or delivered in a vision or in a dream I closely examined everything with the Holy Spirit. I searched for the essence of the message in scripture and noted how each message lined up or didn't line up. I noted whether the context was consistent with the message I received, and whether the message reflected the character and the heart of God. I would ask questions such as "Does this message exalt self, Satan, or God?" This allowed great instructional lessons from the Lord as I began to know His voice on a very intimate level. It is so important to understand that the ability to discern spirits and the messages they bring is a supernatural ability. According to 1 Corinthians 2:14 one cannot discern the things of the spiritual world with his or her natural understanding.

There were times when the Lord needed to deal with some lingering religious mindsets that were preventing me from seeing what was really being said to me— often times this came as an offense. I quickly learned that head knowledge and natural discernment or intuition are not to be trusted and taken for supernatural discernment. Proverbs 14:12 says, "There is a way that seems right to a man, But its end is the way of death." 1 Peter 2:7-8 says, "Therefore, to you who believe, He is precious; but to those who are disobedient, "The stone which the builders rejected has become the chief cornerstone, and "A stone of stumbling And a rock of offense." They stumble, being disobedient to the word, to which they also were appointed." There will be times when the Lord will offend the mind of a person to reveal his or her heart. Even when your mind is offended, however, the words of the Lord will always lead to life, for John 6:62 says, "The words that I speak to you are spirit, and they are life." In fact, this is the point of the offense, to bring a dead and disobedient part of who you are to life and obedience. Remember the story of Naaman in 2 Kings 5?

After determining whether the messages I received were holy or unholy, I waited for confirmation, as 2 Corinthians 13:1 says the Lord will always confirm His words. Waiting on confirmation takes patience and spiritual antennas that are tuned to the Holy Spirit. The Lord delights in revealing Himself in the unexpected and goes for the shock and awe. He has a flair for the dramatic and nothing is off limits; after all, He created *all* things. He delights in the eager expectation of His children who are waiting for Him to speak. This is a patient process of learning and growing, which produces faith—a steady, unwavering belief that the work God starts He will finish. In 2 Timothy 2:15, Paul urges Timothy to "Be *diligent* to present yourself approved to God, a worker who does not need to be ashamed, rightly dividing the word of truth."

What is important to consider here is how the Lord speaks. Not everything is clear. In fact, most is riddled speech. It's layered communication that requires unraveling—much like untying a knot. Much of what the Lord says is multifaceted and there are always at least two ways of viewing each message.

One morning I was praying over this and I saw a gold coin spinning on its side. I heard the

Lord say, "Two sides of the same coin. Two ways to call it: good or evil, heads or tails, positive or negative, light or dark. Call it heads or tails. Coin the phrase." His point was for me to choose my place of viewing. What is your perspective? The way you see God will largely determine your answer to this question. Do you see Him as an untouchable religious being who executes judgment? Or do you see Him as an interactive Father with a tangible presence and a loving heart?

What I have learned is that in all the things God is, He is *love*. He is the perpetual positive being. Everything He does is done through the lens of love with an eternal perspective. 1 Corinthians 13:4-8 says:

> Love suffers long and is kind; love does not envy; love does not parade itself, is not puffed up; does not behave rudely, does not seek its own, is not provoked, thinks no evil; does not rejoice in iniquity, but rejoices in the truth; bears all things, believes all things, hopes all things, endures all things. Love never fails.

This is God!

As you grow in discernment and become increasingly able to thoroughly divide the holy from the unholy, the spiritual food the Lord is giving you increases and the milk turns into solid food. Hebrews 5:14 says, "But solid food belongs to those who are of full age, that is, those who by reason of use have their senses exercised to discern both good and evil."

When the Lord is working within your gifting, teaching you as you go, you will learn in an orderly laid-out manner. Now understand the Lord's idea of learning and growing is not always our understanding. He doesn't wait years for us to *master* something before He advances us—I dare say if He did, we would never get very far, present party included. Rather, He graciously allows us time to absorb and process basic principles and then gently gives us more. It's in the *more* that we learn the prior—it's the application that solidifies an understanding within us.

A Warning about Discerning

It's important to remember that when you discern the spirit inside an individual, do not condemn that person. So much damage has been done to the body of Christ by those who claim they are "discerning the spirits," yet they give way to gossip, assumptions, suspicions, and condemnation. If this is the product of your "discerning," then the wrong spirit is in action because what you're doing is not "discerning the spirits" but judging God's people. This is an area where no Christian should go, for Matthew 7:1-2 says, "Judge not, that you be not judged. For with what judgment you judge, you will be judged; and with the measure you use, it will be measured back to you."

Seeing Demons

"For we do not wrestle against flesh and blood, but against principalities, against powers, against the rulers of the darkness of this age, against spiritual hosts of wickedness in the heavenly places."
(Ephesians 6:12)

After some time of learning the basics of discerning the spiritual atmosphere around me, I started seeing angels and demons. To my surprise, the first place I saw a demon was in church. I know that may shock a good many people, but it's just the truth. In fact, demons are very active in most churches.

The weeklong fall revival of the church we were attending at the time was in full swing. People were being saved and a few had submitted their lives to the ministry. This, as you can imagine, was greatly upsetting to the demonic kingdom.

One night after one of the services, I saw a large demon literally fly into the back of the sanctuary. It was about 12-15 feet tall and stood crouched over. Its wings and body was like those of a bat, and it had short horns all over its head. Its skin was a mixture of black and crimson that looked like crushed velvet when it moved. Its eyes were hollow flames of fire, and its mouth was hollow and black. Such an intense hatred emanated from this being. When it turned and looked directly at me, I literally wanted to crawl under the carpet.

I have since seen this type of demon many times around churches. Several months ago, I was visiting some friends in Chattanooga, Tennessee, and we were going to hear a well-known healing evangelist preach at a local church there. While en route to the church, I glanced out the window of the car and saw four of these demons flying in the same direction we were driving...toward the church. They were flying as though they were late and they were going to be reprimanded for not showing up on time.

When we arrived at the church and were making our way into the sanctuary, I overheard powerful warfare worship that was already underway. *No wonder they were flying so furiously,* I thought.

As we took our seats in the sanctuary, the Lord opened my spiritual eyes to the outside of the church. I saw many of these demons sitting perched along the roof line, as if they were birds on a wire. I asked the Lord, "Why are they there?" The Lord said they were there to steal the word that would be sown that night. Then He led me in prayer for protection over the word that would be delivered so it would be hidden from the birds of the air and they could not steal it. Mark 4:4 says, "And it happened, as he sowed, that some seed fell by the wayside; and the birds of the air came and devoured it." And Job 28:21 says, "It is hidden from the eyes of all living, And concealed from the birds of the air."

Interestingly enough, I have also seen this type of demon chained to the stoop of a building that was once a church in downtown Atlanta, Georgia. It has since been converted to a night club, yet the assignments of the demons had not been re-directed.

This would be quite a long book if I tried to explain every demon I have seen and yet an incomplete one as I see different ones so often. Through the years, I have noticed that demons can take on many different forms and appear as nothing more than a dark hazy fog, to mere blobs with hollow eyes and no nose, to every type of ghoulish figure complete with long teeth, slimy skin, and horns and even cloaked figures, just to name a few. Remember demons are spirits and can morph into whatever shape fits their need. Once on vacation with my family we decided to walk a few blocks into the food district of the marketplace portion of town. As we took to the streets it was still daylight; however, as we began to walk back to our hotel night time had come and darkness had fallen on the city. I began to notice a black fog filtering through corridors of the streets and would dissipate into the alleyways as the nightlife of the city emerged. The area began to take on a completely different feel and I was eager to make it back to our hotel.

On another occasion, one night as I was praying, I had a vision of a demon that was hairy all over and had very long arms that were embracing a person seductively. The demon was standing between the person in the vision and the door that had been opened for me to see him. As I watched the scene play out, I heard the word "seducing." Oddly the demon was wearing a dress. He (or she) turned and saw that I could see him (or her), reached out, and closed the door.

Hmm…. *Well Lord?* I thought. Then I did what I always do and went straight to the Word of God. I found Proverbs 5:20, which says, "For why should you, my son, be enraptured by an immoral woman, And be embraced in the arms of a seductress?" I knew I had to intercede for this person as he or she was being seduced by the enemy.

The predominant power that reigns over the region in which I live is witchcraft, as I have previously mentioned. I will share with you in a couple of sections over how I first came to know this spirit; however, because we are talking about demons here, I want to share with you that during a heightened period of witchcraft activity, the Halloween season, I actually saw this power in its spirit form. On October 12, 2012, I was up very early preparing to meet the Lord in my quiet place when I decided to take my dogs out for a walk first. Upon stepping out of my house, I saw in the spirit gigantic 8 legged creatures literally walking through the region. To compare this thing in size would be like comparing it to a 15-20 story building. I said, "Oh Lord there are spiders walking through the land?" I then heard, "These are not spiders." I instantly knew they were powers and principalities.

I guess one could ask why? What is the benefit of seeing this? Well there are numerous reasons the Lord grants vision to be able to see in the spirit—edification, encouragement, and empowerment. If we believe the Bible when it says in Ephesians 6:12, "For we do not wrestle against flesh and blood, but against principalities, against powers, against the rulers of the darkness of this age, against spiritual hosts of wickedness in the heavenly places." then we can become educated on why we are seeing certain behaviors from people who live in a certain area. The logical thinking is that Powers and Principalities are placed over certain regions and then they affect the people in that area. This is a false thinking. Powers and Principalities are given rights to be enthroned over certain regions or cities because of the decisions of the people who live there. In order to remove the Powers and Principalities you don't fight them but rather you work in tandem with the Holy Spirit to change the hearts of the people who live in that area. When the thinking is shifted the Powers or Principalities are removed because they no longer have a legal right to be there. This knowledge is empowering and can produce change.

The Last Enemy to be Destroyed

There is one demonic spirit I want to mention before moving on and that is the spirit of Death. 1 Corinthians 15:26 says, "The last enemy that will be destroyed is death". I encountered this spirit for the first time 10 years ago, and since that time, I seem to be seeing it more and more often. 1 Corinthians 15:26 says, 'The last enemy that will be destroyed is death." Most certainly, the frequency of seeing this demon has to do with the times we are in. With the widely acclaimed vampire media, which embodies and glorifies the spirit of Death, the world is setting the stage to receive this spirit through desensitization. This is the counterfeit move the enemy is making by distorting 1 Corinthians 15:53-54:

> For this corruptible must put on incorruption, and this mortal must put on immortality. So when this corruptible has put on incorruption, and this mortal has put on immortality, then shall be brought to pass the saying that is written: "Death is swallowed up in victory."

In its spirit form, Death looks a lot like what the world calls "the grim reaper," a black cloaked body with a white skull face, who comes only to steal your destiny but he may also steal the destiny of others through you or your lineage. Remember why the enemy comes: to steal, kill, and destroy.

The first time I encountered this spirit was in a dream. I saw what looked like a small village and a black cloaked white skull-faced spirit making its rounds from house to house. I would hear gut-wrenching screams as the spirit entered each house. While I was standing in the doorway of one of the homes, the spirit passed by, simply looked at me, and went to the next house. Only a couple of nights later, I was working the night shift at the hospital and in the wee hours of the morning I stepped out of the nurse's station to make rounds. At the end of the long hallway, I saw a black cloaked, white skulled-face figure. The third time I saw it, it literally morphed out of the body of an elderly lady. Sadly about a week later, I heard she had passed away from cancer. After this third encounter I realized this was the spirit of death I was seeing and this realization brought me to my knees before the Lord. I received a strong warning from the Lord that day as He said sternly, "Never speak death over anyone. Only speak life!" I came to understand that day I would encounter this spirit many more times in my life and these instructions from the Lord would prove crucial.

The Word of God says we hold the power of life and death in our tongues—this is the power in our words. One night as I was praying I had a vision of an older fella I knew. I saw the outside of his home, and peering around the edge of it was the spirit of Death looking at me. I made a point to go see this older gentleman the next day, and sure enough, his conversation was all about dying, as it always was. Now this man was not suicidal—he didn't want to die. In fact, he really wanted to live and was having a hard time accepting the aging process.

When he started his "death talk," I immediately, yet politely, interrupted him. I told them that for someone who wanted to live, he sure talked about dying a lot. I told him about the power of our words and how our tongues have the power to produce life OR death. His wife was sitting nearby with a big smile on her face, agreeing with the turn of the conversation. I asked him if he believed in Jesus. He shook his head yes and said, "I go to church every Sunday."

I said, "Well...then do you believe your Bible?"

Once again, he shook his head yes in agreement.

I said, "Well then you must believe it when it says that life and death is in the power of the tongue."

He looked at me for a good 15 to 20 seconds and finally said, "Well yes it does. You're right."

Then I suggested that instead of speaking about death all the time that we speak life into our day. "Would that be all right?" I asked.

He looked at me a bit stunned and said, "Yes, that would be okay."

I then asked if I could pray for him.

He said, "Well, please pray for me; I need it."

I couldn't help but smile at this precious elderly fella. So I prayed for him, declaring that death and all conversation of death was hereby null and void and could no longer have any influence on this man or his family in Jesus' name. I then began to declare life over him and his household in Jesus' name. It was a precious day. His wife was so grateful because she was so tired of hearing him talk about death all the time.

Seeing Spiritual Things

"But as it is written: "Eye has not seen, nor ear heard, Nor have entered into the heart of man The things which God has prepared for those who love Him." But God has revealed them to us through His Spirit. For the Spirit searches all things, yes, the deep things of God." (1 Corinthians 2:9-10)

The spiritual realm is not a void of vast empty spaces. On the contrary, in fact, the spiritual realm is layered dimensions with hidden treasures that are just wanting to be discovered—and received. The things which God has prepared for those who love Him are many—for He is a Father who loves to give.

By the time I began seeing spiritual objects or things I guess you could say I had become used to the spiritual realm and the seemingly random unpredictable appearances of sudden flashes of light, angels, and demons. So, suddenly seeing a pile of gold coins, stairways, vases of oil, golden crowns, etc., seemed to be oddly normal. Speaking of gold coins, I have seen large piles of these beside people who have great spiritual wealth available to them or whom God is entrusting with actual wealth for kingdom purposes. One in particular that I am reminded of right now is a middle-aged gentleman I met recently. He is the son of one who spends his life sowing wealth into the kingdom of God. As a result, he and the generations that are following him are reaping wealth in the way of finances and astounding spiritual gifts. You see, we were never meant to live life as paupers and beggars. Jesus came so that we could live life abundantly (John 10:10). That's not a "name it and claim it" doctrine; it's just biblical truth.

    I have seen rivers and waterfalls in churches and in homes where the Holy Spirit is welcomed and honored all the time.

    I have seen angels bring huge jugs and vats of oil of healing and restoration into sanctuaries to pour on people during worship. I am reminded of a certain weekend I was visiting a friend's church in East Georgia. A well-known prophet and his wife were there ministering. As they were speaking, I saw a tall slender angel wearing a white and the palest of blue flowing robe suddenly appear carrying a vase of oil that was almost as tall as she was. Honestly, I have no idea how she lifted it. She did, however, quite easily and poured the golden oil over a young man sitting two rows in front of me. When the service was over I approached him and shared with him what I saw. Much to my surprise he was elated and began shouting and jumping in excitement. Through his jubilant expressions I managed to learn that he was an evangelist that has been asking for a fresh anointing—well he got it!

    One Sunday evening I was attending a church about an hour from my home. After the service I was talking with a precious lady who I could tell by her physical appearance had lived a rough life. Inwardly, however, she was radiant. She had a spiritual glow that was illuminating the room. The more this lady shared with me the more I began to see in the spirit a golden crown appear on her head. I, to this day, cannot remember a thing she said to me as I was overwhelmed at her spiritual appearance. I learned from her pastor later that she only one week prior received salvation, which was a huge feat for her. I learned that she had endured through great struggles in many areas of her life in order to just believe. This lady was precious to the Lord. He had seen every struggle and walked with her through every battle. This golden crown was the crown of life (James 1:12).

I was attending a "Hearing God's Voice" class one Friday night in South Alabama when I met a sweet, angelic-faced young lady. She was very humble in her countenance yet in the spirit she was a fierce warrior. As I stepped forward in a prophetic exercise, I saw her in the spirit wearing a suit of armor that looked as though it was made of heavy-duty steel that had been hammered to perfection. From head to toe this armor was studded in diamonds. Every inch of this young lady was covered in armor—I tell you absolutely nothing was getting through this suit. She mounted a barded horse whose armor was exactly like hers. She carried a sword as large as a javelin. Later in talking with her I learned that she was once a high-ranking witch. Now, however, she is a mighty warrior for Jesus Christ and a valued weapon in His arsenal. Praise the Lord!

On many occasions I have seen stairways descend into sanctuaries and watched as angels descend and ascend them, carrying large bowls to collect the worship. I have even seen Jesus descend and walk among the people, ministering to them personally as they worshipped and poured out their hearts to Him. Contrary to what some believe, Jesus is not glued to His throne. His heart is for His people and He *loves* to minister directly to them. He loves to inhabit the praises of His people as recorded in Psalm 22:3. I jokingly say that when Jesus shows up, He comes dressed for the occasion. Several years back, I visited one of my favorite churches in South Alabama, Revival Central Ministries for All Nations. They have a highly anointed flag ministry called Blessed Hands. Prior to their performance we were in congregational worship when Apostle Dennis Arnold acknowledged that he heard the angels declare "The King draws nigh." Just moments later I saw Jesus descend with many angels flanking His right and left sides. He was wearing a long white robe with a crimson red sash over His shoulder, extending to his waist. After worship, the flag ministry took the stage and I was shocked to see that for their first performance, their flags were white and crimson red.

I have seen brick walls around people that are often erected by their own choosing to protect a broken heart. Unfortunately these walls also prevent healing and restoration as the enemy establishes a fortress to hold the broken heart captive.

I have seen brick walls in churches where the Holy Spirit is not allowed to work. Most often these are due to religious doctrines and traditions that place limits on the spirituality of the church. This is a grievous thing.

I have seen the anointing fall upon congregations in many forms, as the worship touches the heart of God. While often times it is a light mist that falls, at other times, it can be as powerful as a deluge.

I have seen transparent domes over churches and homes, which means the inheritances of the inhabitants are protected from the enemy for kingdom purposes. There is one of these domes covering a small Baptist church near my home that is being more sensitive to the move the Holy Spirit than the dictated doctrines of religion.

Many times I have seen the accuser of the brethren dressed in a black robe and a black and dark crimson king's crown petition God in a courtroom. The accuser is Satan and we are to *never* stand in his place (Revelation 12:10). The children of God are to *never* stand and accuse their brothers or sisters in Christ. When we do, we are standing in the place of Satan. If you take this position, you will not fare well.

I have seen daggers and swords protruding out of the backs and necks of people. There is truth to the phrase "being stabbed in the back." These are often there from negative words spoken by others. Sometimes, however, these are self-inflicting.

The Lord said to me once that when we speak life – life happens. Then He showed me a person speaking, and as the person spoke, a river flowing with life floating on melodies of rainbows proceeded out of their mouth. This river floated out and up. Carried on this river was every good thing: love, joy, happiness, peace, laughter, shields, even birds which represents songs and butterflies which can represent several things: speaking change, speaking in the spirit, and even a new creation. When we speak "life" life happens! Ephesians 5:19 says, "Speaking to one another in psalms and hymns and spiritual songs, singing and making melody in your heart to the Lord."

Then I saw a person speaking words that produced death and as the person spoke I saw a black river flowing out and downward. I saw on this river garbage, sewage, waste, daggers, and words such as inequity, curses, lies, hate, unbelief, and slander. As the person spoke, some of the words would fall to the ground, becoming stumbling blocks or word hindrances for themselves and others while other words, however, would soar through the air and become swords and daggers and inflict pain and curses on others. These daggers and swords remain stuck in the people until the words or curses are broken and removed.

Recently, I attended a deliverance meeting conducted by Jay Bartlett where a demon was made to remove all the swords and daggers that it had inflicted on the person in Jesus' name. The demon literally pulled out swords and daggers for twenty minutes. (Leviticus 19:14; Isaiah 57:14; Jeremiah 6:21; Ezekiel 3:20; 7:19; Zephaniah 1:3; Romans 11:9; Romans 14:13; 1 Corinthians 1:23; 1 Corinthians 8:9; Revelation 2:14).

I have seen chains bound around heads where the enemy has bound people's minds. These are strongholds and unholy mindsets.

I could go on and on, but before I move on, I would like to mention one demonic thing I encounter a good bit—spiders. As I previously mentioned, spiders in the Spirit represent witchcraft.

The first time I saw a spiritual spider was in a vision. I was reaching out to grab a handle of a pot when I heard "Watch your fingers." I removed my hand and looked on the underside of the handle to find a big black spider hiding there. The Lord was teaching me that even though I would encounter things that looked normal, they contain the under workings of witchcraft—the enemy—and I am to not touch such evil things. What was interesting is that I had just started attending a small ministry group that would later prove to be run by a highly controlling and manipulative leader.

Similarly, in another experience, I saw in the Spirit a grasshopper. As I watched it, it turned into a spider, and I heard, "Things are not always as they seem." There are things that seem very small and insignificant, and yet they are very deadly. Proverbs 14:12 says, "There is a way that seems right to a man, But its end is the way of death."

The Bible says these things about witchcraft, spiders' webs, and those who weave them:

- Deuteronomy 18:10: "There shall not be found among you anyone who makes his son or his daughter pass through the fire, or one who practices witchcraft, or a soothsayer, or one who interprets omens, or a sorcerer,"

- 1 Samuel 15:23: "For rebellion is as the sin of witchcraft, And stubbornness is as iniquity and idolatry. Because you have rejected the word of the Lord, He also has rejected you from being king."

- 2 Kings 9:22: 'Now it happened, when Joram saw Jehu, that he said, 'Is it peace, Jehu?' So he answered, 'What peace, as long as the harlotries of your mother Jezebel and her witchcraft are so many?'"

- Isaiah 59:-5-6: "No one calls for justice, Nor does any plead for truth. They trust in empty words and speak lies; They conceive evil and bring forth iniquity. They hatch vipers' eggs and weave the spider's web; He who eats of their eggs dies, And from that which is crushed a viper breaks out. Their webs will not become garments, Nor will they cover themselves with their works; Their works are works of iniquity, And the act of violence is in their hands."

A Word About Rebellion

"For rebellion is as the sin of witchcraft." The root word for "rebellion" is *marah*[iii] and it means "to be bitter; to rebel or resist:—bitter, change, be disobedient, disobey, grievously, provocation, provoke(ing)." There are those who literally practice witchcraft with spells and curses, but yet there is another type of witchcraft that many Christians practice every day by merely walking in disobedience.

The sin of disobedience is as the sin of witchcraft. If we are not continually walking toward God in the calling and destiny *He* ordained for us from the foundation of the world, then we are walking in rebellion and disobedience—witchcraft. If we are not loving our neighbor, then we are walking in rebellion and disobedience—witchcraft! For the greatest commandment is "To love thy neighbor as yourself!"

If you are trying to control or manipulate others through your words or actions, you are using witchcraft. This, unfortunately, is a very serious problem even within the body of Christ. Pastors and teachers fall prey to this witchcraft spirit way too often.

Once I was visiting a small church and upon arriving there, several members approached me asking me to please petition the Lord regarding what was going on in their church. They explained to me that many people visit their church; however, they couldn't seem to get them to stay. I was perplexed at first by this because on the surface this church was very welcoming and personable; however, I was drawn to simply listen to the words of the pastor. I began to notice that much of his speech even from the pulpit was controlling in nature. He would use phrases such as "Now I am your pastor and I am telling you...." Hmm...that seemed to alert my spiritual antennas. So, I went to the Lord in prayer over this situation asking the Lord to please reveal the root of what was going on in this church. Within minutes I saw in the spirit a big black spider sitting on my right shoulder. Immediately I knew that the root of the problems within this church was witchcraft, even Jezebel, and it was stemming from the authority in the church—the pastor. I also knew from this vision that the pastor had been approached with this before and he would not listen to the correction. Nehemiah 9:29 says, "And testified against them, That You might bring them back to Your law. Yet they acted proudly, And did not heed your commandments, But sinned against Your judgments, Which if a man does, he shall live by them. And they shrugged their shoulders, and stiffened their necks, And would not hear."

For a short season, I was being mentored by a Christian lady. As time progressed, I began to learn that she was very controlling and was unwilling to deviate from her mindsets. Because of these mindsets, however, I began to struggle with my gifting and doubt began to overtake me. I would, so often, cry out to the Lord in prayer asking for the root of my struggles and in return I began to be flooded with visions and dreams of spiders. The word "mentor" actually means "teacher." James 3:1 says, "My brethren, let not many of you become teachers, knowing that we shall receive a stricter judgment." The reason teachers will receive a stricter judgment than those they are teaching is because they can influence a thought pattern—they can create mindsets. Proverbs 23:7 says, "For as he thinks in his heart, so is he..." That word "think" is *sha'ar* in Hebrew which means to split or open or act as a gatekeeper. Our thoughts act as gatekeepers into our hearts. Thoughts can turn into mindsets and mindsets can turn into strongholds, which demons can attach themselves to. In turn if faulty mindsets or unholy mindsets are established, destinies can be altered. The responsibility of being a teacher or a mentor is not to be taken lightly.

The problem with this mentor was that every time I shared the dreams and visions that revealed the plans of the enemy, she always told me they were not from the Lord. She told me I was seeing the demonic because I had opened the door to the enemy. This confused me greatly as I live a carefully sanctified lifestyle, guarding my eyes, ears, and relationships very closely. In fact, I pray the blood of Jesus over my visions, dreams, eyes, and ears daily. I remembered the word from the Lord when He told me He would reveal the plans of the enemy to me. Yet this mentor was "teaching" me that God was not showing me these evil plans. I had become conflicted and burdened because I respected and trusted her greatly.

One morning during this burdensome time, I was pouring my coffee and setting my heart on worship when the Lord said to me, "I have much to tell you, but you must lose some weight first." Knowing the Lord speaks in riddles, I knew the word "weight" did not mean physical weight. It meant "burdens," and I instantly saw this lady's face before me. I knew the time had come where I had to separate myself from her if I were going to be obedient to my specific calling as a Seer. So I asked the Lord to please provide the opportunity for me to separate from her, and sure enough, He did—and He did it quickly. After we parted, all my visions and dreams of spiders immediately stopped. In fact, an entire year passed without me having one dream or vision of a spider.

God's Seers are on the front lines of the battle, and the Lord is continually revealing the plans of the enemy to them. Much of what Seers receive is demonic in nature simply because that is who we are fighting against. It is the Lord who reveals the enemy's plans to us, however.

I was reading one of Wendy Alac's books, titled *Visions from Heaven,* recently and was elated when I read these words:

> In fact, many of these prophets, seers, and intercessors had been to the enemy's own war rooms, undetected. And were devastating to the enemy's plans. Stopping them at every turn. They were greatly hated and feared by the enemy.

I have met so many in the body of Christ who want to act as though the dark side doesn't exist, however, in doing this they are actually embracing it. It's turning a blind eye and meanwhile the enemy is ravishing the church. Christians, we must not be afraid to get down and dirty in this fight with the enemy. He is constantly raging a war against you and all that the Lord has called you to do for the kingdom of God. Matthew 11:12 says, "And from the days of John the Baptist until now the kingdom of heaven suffers violence, and the violent take it by force."

Seeing Angels

"Are they not all ministering spirits sent forth to minister for those who will inherit salvation?"
(Hebrews 1:14)

The first time I saw an angel in full form was bit of a welcome surprise, especially after seeing so many demons. I had just arrived home and was completely exhausted from a long day at work. I grabbed a bottle of water and made my way to our screened-in porch. As I sat relaxed, suddenly a storm erupted out of the North, complete with lightning and strong winds. Then, right before my eyes, lightning struck and a strong wind blew down a tree about 25 feet from where I was sitting, knocking out the power line as it fell. *Great!* I thought. *What a perfect end to a perfect day.* I got up, made my way to the sofa, and fell asleep. About 30 minutes later, I woke only to see an angel kneeling beside me. He was wearing a khaki-colored tunic and had blond curly hair and clear blue eyes. He had somewhat of a boyish face and smiled preciously as we made eye contact. Then he softly faded away.

Just days later, I saw another angel in full form. He was gold from head to toe, literally—radiantly stunning! Everything about him was golden—his eyes, his skin, even his hair, which was short gold curls. He was about 6 to 7 feet tall and had a beautiful face with dimples and a huge smile. He was also quite muscular. At the time I met him, he was carrying an armload of trumpet sea shells and handed them to me. I later learned these sea shells were for hearing in the spirit.

Psalms 91:10-11 says, "No evil shall befall you, Nor shall any plague come near your dwelling; For He shall give His angels charge over you, To keep you in all your ways." More and more often I began to see the same angel hanging around me—I will call him my guardian angel. Through the years I have watched my angel change as I have changed. When I saw him early in my gifting, he wasn't adorned with much other than a sword. As I have grown and matured in my gifting, however, I have watched as he has also become more adorned and grown in stature and strength.

Earlier this year, I dreamed a beautiful red-haired angel, named Wisdom, adorned in rubies (Proverbs 8:11), handed me a large emerald clutch covered in what looked like glittering sequins. I took it in my hands and said, "Wow, there is so much depth to this color. It is gorgeous." Then I handed it back to her. She took it, placed it back in my hands firmly, and said, "Yes, it is. Make double emerald. This is huge!"

The Hebrew word *bareqeth*[iv] means "a gem (as flashing), perhaps the emerald—carbuncle." It comes from the Hebrew word *baraq*[v] which means "a flashing sword—bright, glitter (-ing sword), lightning." Ever since Wisdom placed this glittering sword in my hands, I have seen my angel adorned with emeralds around his neck.

Aside from his armor, my angel carries a quiver-type satchel on his back. In it he carries tools I need to accomplish my destiny. One of these tools is a chisel. He says that I, along with many others, have been given the task to bring down a wall.

I have since learned the Lord assigned this angel to me when He opened my spiritual eyes. His assignment is to protect all matters of my heart. For a Seer, the eyes of the heart is of utmost importance. One doesn't see in the Spirit with his or her natural eyes; it is with the eyes of the heart that one is granted access to view the spiritual realms. Ephesians 1:18 says, "I pray that the eyes of your heart may be enlightened in order that you may know the hope to which he has called you, the riches of his glorious inheritance in his holy people,"

A Word of Caution

I want to issue a caution here. It is a grievous thing to place more emphasis on angelic beings than on the Holy Spirit. Angels are created beings, and there is much to be said about them and the work they do on the earth. They take their jobs very seriously. In fact, we are their jobs. We employ them. Hebrews 1:14 says God created them to minister to those who are to inherit salvation. When we are going about our kingdom assignments, our angels are hard at work right along with us. Our prayers, our words, empower them to act.

Angels have delivered messages to me from God and are careful to advise that the words they speak are not their own, but God's. Once I wanted to verify that a message I received was from the Lord, so I asked my angel if he was the one who delivered that particular message to me. He said, "It was my voice but God's words."

Aside from delivering messages, they help in many other ways, as well. I have been in deliverance meetings where angels have held demons at sword's point as the man or woman of God conducting the meeting commanded the demons to obey in the name of Jesus.

I have watched as angels collect worship from congregations in large vats or bowls, ascend into heaven, and carry them to the throne of God.

I have watched as one stands and testifies to the goodness of the Lord and his or her angel stands right beside them-listening intently with such compassionate expressions.

Angels are very active in our lives and often bring us gifts from God, just as the golden angel brought me trumpet sea shells. But they also deliver mantels, robes, tools, and other objects to help us in our callings.

Looking into the Spirit

"That the God of our Lord Jesus Christ, the Father of glory, may give to you the spirit of wisdom and revelation in the knowledge of Him, the eyes of your understanding being enlightened; that you may know what is the hope of His calling, what are the riches of the glory of His inheritance in the saints,"

(Ephesians 1:16-18)

     Several years after I started having visions and dreams, the visions seemed to fade in frequency for a time. I began to worry that I had done something to inhibit the flow or that the Lord had changed His mind about revealing His word to me in this way. The Holy Spirit gently reminded me, however, of Romans 11:29: "For the gifts and the calling of God are irrevocable." This means God doesn't take them back. So, having that settled in my heart, I simply asked the Lord, "What is going on? Why were the visions becoming less?"

     In response, He showed me a golden light switch and said, "I want to teach you how to turn the switch on and off."

Hmm...well that would be nice, I thought. I would soon learn, however, that this was harder than it sounded and that it would take greater faith to graduate to this level. It's one thing to simply have something flash before your eyes. It's quite a different ballgame to ask the Lord to reveal something, press in to receive it, and have the faith to act on it.

Ephesians 1:18 says, "the eyes of your understanding being enlightened; that you may know what is the hope of His calling, what are the riches of the glory of His inheritance in the saints." The word "understanding" in Greek is dianoia[vi], which means "deep thought, imagination, mind, understanding." So, this verse could read "the eyes of your imagination being enlightened." Seeing or looking into the spirit is receiving through the imagination.

The way the Lord started teaching me how to utilize my imagination was through discernment—a supernatural knowing that something is there. If you will remember, discernment was one of the first things the Lord taught me as it is a foundational key from which to build. As with anything, the foundation has to be well placed or everything will get skewed.

The imagination is simply a way of receiving information, much like a television or a radio. These are the conduits, not the source. When you watch television, you're not seeing something being produced by the television. The source of what you're seeing may be happening thousands of miles away and the television is just the means by which you are viewing it. The imagination works in the same way; it is just a means by which the Lord can download information.

This way of receiving is more initiated by the Seer. It's like choosing a program to watch from your television's program guide. In other words, I can scan the room and discern a lot of angelic or demonic activity, but I may choose to zero in on one particular person to look deeper into the spiritual atmosphere around him or her. If I do this, I will see the angel or demon next to him or her in detail. Or I might see that this person already has arrows in his or her back or a lock over his or her heart. This was a bit hard for me to grasp at first, but the Lord was very patient in confirming everything to me. Eventually, over time, I began to just trust and flow in this level of faith. Now in addition to dreams and visions, I can choose to turn on the "television" of my imagination and see in the Spirit anytime I want.

One day I was talking to a friend on the phone about pressing into the Spirit to see deeper. She explained to me that she only sees flashes of light and dark and wanted to know how to see in more detail.

I began to explain that seeing flashes of light and dark shadows are only surface-type stuff—they are only indications that something more is present. It's the bated hook that makes you want to bite. You can choose to go deeper by simply looking should you have the faith. I read somewhere that mustard-seed faith is not the faith that heals someone; it is the faith it takes to simply pray the prayer to begin with. In the same way, the faith it takes to see in the Spirit is simply the faith that believes you can and then choosing to look. Faith is always an action word.

As we were talking about this, I keep hearing the words, "Look again." And the scripture that was being replayed in my thoughts is of the time when Jesus healed the blind man at Bethsaida in Mark 8:22-25:

> Then He came to Bethsaida; and they brought a blind man to Him, and begged Him to touch him. So He took the blind man by the hand and led him out of the town. And when He had spit on his eyes and put His hands on him, He asked him if he saw anything. And he looked up and said, "I see men like trees, walking." Then He put His hands on his eyes again and made him look up. And he was restored and saw everyone clearly.

There is so much richness to this story. Sometimes we aren't able to see simply because of our surroundings—our lives are too worldly; sometimes we refuse to be led by the Spirit; and other times we only have to press in and simply look again.

There are times when God only shows me a shadow of what is there. If I choose to look deeper, I can, and when I do, I see details and not just flashes, shadows, or blobs of color.

During our phone conversation, as we were talking about looking deeper, suddenly before me stood an angel. I was so taken by his presence and his agenda that upon seeing him I received an understanding of his purpose. I immediately shared with a friend that an angel was standing before me and he wanted me to ask her to describe him. He was so excited to aid us in our discussion and be a tool of demonstration. I thanked the Father for sending one of His angels to help me describe how to look deeper and then asked my friend to close her eyes and visualize the angel standing before me. Even though we live about 300 miles apart, the spiritual realm knows no distance. So all she needed to do was put her faith in action. She needed to choose to look beyond her own dimension or environment and focus her spiritual eyes on the angel standing in front of me. She then said, "I see blue and white but I can't make out much else."

I wanted to encourage her right away that she was seeing the angel in order to lift her level of faith and give her the boost to go deeper. So I shared with her that she was seeing correctly as the angel was wearing a blue sash across his shoulder, which extended down to his waist, along with a white kilt-type skirt.

She erupted with excitement and, I might add, the angel was also enjoying this lesson very much. Then I asked her to focus her spiritual eyes on the details, which means choosing to look into the depths. In other words, I was asking her to look again and describe what she was seeing. She then said he had curly blonde hair and was smiling a goofy smile from ear to ear. "He is really enjoying this," she said. "YES! Exactly!" I said. She'd perfectly described what the angel looked like. Now I asked her to open her eyes and look beyond the natural in front of her and see the angel with her spiritual eyes having her natural eyes open. She was so excited to share that she was able to see the angel with her eyes open.

Once I was talking to a young man who was sharing with me about his ailing father. As he was going on and on about his dad, I sensed a demonic presence. I chose to look into the Spirit and I saw a demon attached to this man—literally hanging around his neck. As soon as I saw the demon, it started talking to me in a language I didn't understand, which I found quite irritating. So, I simply told the demon to be quiet in Jesus' name and it stopped talking. I was able to gather that it was a demon of control who was influencing the son to execute power over his father. So I asked the Father, "What do you want me to do about this demon?"

"Nothing. Ignore it and empower the dad," He responded.

So that is what I did. I met with the dad and began speaking words of empowerment over him. He seemed so shocked that I was talking to him and not his son. The more I empowered him through positive words, however, the more I saw his face soften and he began to open up to me about what was going on in his heart.

This past summer at The School of The Prophets conducted by Prophetess Jan Porubsky, as a speaker was giving a powerful rhema word, I asked the Lord what was going on around her that she could deliver such a powerful word. Immediately I saw two angels, one standing on either side of her. The one standing on her right was reading to her from a book. The one on her left was writing the words she was saying. Every now and then the one on her left glanced up to the Father with a smile on his face and said, "She is spot on." Later, as were breaking for lunch, the Lord said to me, "Would you like to bless her?"

I said, "Oh Lord, yes I would."

He said, "Well why don't you share with her what you saw while she was speaking?"

So, while we were eating, I asked her if she would like to know what I saw while she was speaking."

She smiled very big and said, "Yes I would!"

Then I shared with her exactly what I saw. What's interesting is that the Lord had been talking to her about speaking and teaching extemporaneously, trusting Him to give her the words without notes or quotes. So He instructed me to encourage her and build her faith by sharing with her what I saw in the Spirit. Before she ever got up to speak, He delivered the words she was about to say to His angels. She was elated and greatly encouraged.

Being able to see this way simply means exercising a particular spiritual muscle. I remember about five years ago I received an instant message from Mike Rogers, Senior Pastor at New Bern Church in North Carolina. I had just completed a blog radio interview and Mike sent me a message asking if I had ever utilized the door in Revelation 4. Completely intrigued, I quickly responded that I had not but I wanted to know what he knew about that door and how I could use it. He simply said, "Ask the Father to show you the door in Revelation 4." That was it. I laughed and said something like, "Okay, well, ask and you shall receive...Father, can I see the door in Revelation 4?" As I watched a door appeared to me in the spirit.

I was so excited that I sent Pastor Mike a message telling him I was seeing the door. He said, "Well, go through it and tell me what you see." So, I did! And wow! What I saw was simply amazing to me. I saw rolling hills of the most vibrant green grass I had ever seen and fruit trees lining a crystal river that sparkled like diamonds. I walked up to one of the fruit trees and observed the fruit. Each piece was huge and perfectly ripe. Scanning the area, I saw a group of people wearing long, white robes, standing under one of the fruit trees about 25 yards away. I turned to look at the fruit, then turned back to look at the people, and I noticed someone was walking toward me. Slightly freaking out, I shared this with Pastor Mike. What he said next shocked me: "I see him," he said. "I am standing in the group of people under the fruit tree." *What?* I thought. He can see everything I can see? I had no time to even ponder that before this gentleman walking toward me was standing with me with his arm across my shoulder. He had dark hair and a beard. It was Joshua. He didn't tell me his name but rather I simply knew it. He asked if he could pray for me. Just then, Pastor Mike said, "Erica, He is imparting boldness. Receive it." After Joshua prayed for me, he picked a piece of fruit from the tree we were standing under and handed it to me. I took a bite of it. It had an odd texture. In a way, it looked like a grapefruit but had the texture of an avocado. Joshua smiled very big and walked away; then the vision ended. I was absolutely speechless. I mean what am I supposed to say after something like that happens? All I could think of was "Oh my goodness."

That evening, as I was pondering this vision before the Lord, I asked if there was a scripture that supported what I had experienced. Audibly I heard:

"But you have come to Mount Zion and to the city of the living God, the heavenly Jerusalem, to an innumerable company of angels, to the general assembly and church of the firstborn who are registered in heaven, to God the Judge of all, to the spirits of just men made perfect, to Jesus the Mediator of the new covenant, and to the blood of sprinkling that speaks better things than that of Abel." I immediately recognized this as coming from Hebrews—Hebrews 12:22-24.

I have since utilized this door many times.

Through the years of seeing this way, I have learned it really is the grace of God that He gives an on and off switch. It is a gift, an invitation that says you are welcome here anytime. It is the perfect medium for living life with no visual access to the spiritual realm verses seeing life completely in both the natural and the spiritual realms at one time. This is called open vision; however, it involves much more than vision as all of the senses are involved. After only a couple of experiences with this, I quickly learned that living life this way would be extremely difficult. Open vision allows you to experience all of the body's senses in both the natural and the spiritual realms all at once as they are literally transposed over one another. It is very difficult to distinguish what is happening in the natural and what is happening in the spiritual.

What should be remembered is that it is God who gives access to experience the fullness of the treasures that He has hidden for all of His children. We only have to want to take the key and open the door or turn on the switch to see all that He has for us. Remember seeing in the Spirit is a gift, and God wants us all to enjoy what He has given us.

Receiving Beforehand

"Now I tell you before it comes, that when it does come to pass, you may believe that I am He." (John 13:19)

I began to notice that there were times when prior to arriving at a specific place, God might give me a vision of a person who will be there or He might show me the spiritual atmosphere of the place I am going.

Recently, I was getting ready to leave my home and visit a church I had not attended in about a month. Suddenly a vision of the church's sanctuary flashed before my eyes. Along the back wall of the sanctuary, I saw angels and demons just standing there. None of them were doing anything.

When I arrived at the church and the service was underway, I found out why. The service was as dry as a potato chip. The songs the worship leaders sang were completely absent of any anointing. The people were thinking of everything but worship. Literally, they were going through the motions of Sunday morning worship, yet they had the blankest expressions on their faces. The Lord reminded me of Matthew 15:8: "These people draw near to Me with their mouth, And honor Me with their lips, But their heart is far from Me." It was painful to watch.

Finally, the worship leaders started singing a song that was inviting to the Holy Spirit. A shift happened. I saw the anointing begin to fall. It was like a dam had opened and a river of living water was now flowing into the sanctuary. I praised the Lord for this release, yet after one verse and chorus the song ended. Oh, the spirit was so grieved. I began to ask the Lord what was going on because I had just been to this church a month prior and the worship was so anointed. The presence of the Lord was so powerful. Just then I heard the Lord say "the mic." Then I noticed the pastor was not there. Just then the speakers for the morning service announced the pastor and his wife were out of town. The Lord said, "Here is the message for the pastor. Tell him I want to take his ministry to the next level. I have big plans for this church but the mic has to be protected." There is an anointing that must be protected and the Holy Spirit will not rest on just anyone or any church.

I sent a message to the pastor and told him I was standing in his church. I then asked him if he wanted to know what I was seeing. He immediately responded, "Yes!" So I told him I would call him after the service. When the service ended and I called the pastor, I shared with him the vision I had prior to my arrival and then what I saw and heard during the service. He was shocked at the timing as he had just gotten off the phone with the prophet of the house who told him, "The Lord is getting ready to expand the walls of your church and there won't be enough room for all the people. You're going to have to add on."

I laughed and said, "Well, there you go, out of the mouths of two." He was very appreciative of my call.

Section Three:
Hearing in the Spirit

Hearing Angels

"But as it is written: 'Eye has not seen, nor ear heard, Nor have entered into the heart of man The things which God has prepared for those who love Him.' But God has revealed them to us through His Spirit. For the Spirit searches all things, yes, the deep things of God." (1 Corinthians 2:9-10)

*"I will stand my watch
And set myself on the rampart,
And watch to see what He will say to me, And what I will answer when I am corrected."
(Habakkuk 2:1)*

About two weeks after the golden angel gave me the armload of trumpet sea shells, I dreamed I saw a local pastor behind the pulpit. As I was watching him, in my dream, I not only heard him preaching but I also heard his spirit speaking. The following night I had the same dream. I saw the same pastor preaching, and as I was watching him preach, I heard both him and his spirit speaking simultaneously. Each time the spirit spoke, however, I heard it in an unknown language. This time I was posed this question at the end of the dream: "Is it possible for you to hear the spirit of a man?" Then I woke up. *Hmm...well, Lord, this is different*, I thought. Pondering the question, my mind rapidly searched through the scriptures and I remembered Mark 9:23 and 1 Corinthians 2:9-10:

- Mark 9:23 says, "Jesus said to him, 'If you can believe, all things are possible to him who believes."

- 1 Corinthians 2:9-10 says, "But as it is written: 'Eye has not seen, nor ear heard, Nor have entered into the heart of man The things which God has prepared for those who love Him.' But God has revealed them to us through His Spirit. For the Spirit searches all things, yes, the deep things of God."

So, I thought that if everything is possible to him who believes, then my answer would have to be yes. My reply to the Lord, however, was much like Ezekiel's when God asked him if the dry bones could live: "Oh Lord only you know." Here is a tip. If the Lord ever asks you a question like the one He asked me, just answer, "Oh Lord only you know" because you honestly have no idea what He is about to do (smile)!

Hebrews 4:12 says: "For the word of God is living and powerful, and sharper than any two-edged sword, piercing even to the division of soul and spirit, and of joints and marrow, and is a discerner of the thoughts and intents of the heart."

2 Kings 6:12 says: "And one of his servants said, 'None, my lord, O king; but Elisha, the prophet who is in Israel, tells the king of Israel the words that you speak in your bedroom.'"

Job 4:12 says: "Now a word was secretly brought to me, And my ear received a whisper of it."

I quickly discovered that it is possible to hear the spirit of man, as I will share about that a bit later, but I also learned that the ability to hear in the Spirit applies to the spiritual realm as a whole as I began to hear angels and demons talking. I often will wake during the night and hear angels discussing their assignments from God. I have heard them worshiping the Father and I have heard my own spirit conversing in peaceful communion with the trinity.

One morning as I was worshiping the Lord, I suddenly saw the room fill with angels. Some had instruments such as harps and trumpets. As I worshiped I could also hear them worshiping—in song. That was a good morning (smile).

Most often when I hear angels, I hear their voices through my spiritual ears without seeing their mouths move. Sometimes it's like hearing a voice in my thoughts and knowing I didn't just think it with my mind. This communication is unmistakable because angels don't talk like you or I; they often speak in word puns, riddles, or dark speech because they are simply delivering the words of God. Numbers 12:6-8 says:

> Then He said, "Hear now My words: If there is a prophet among you, I, the Lord, make Myself known to him in a vision; I speak to him in a dream. Not so with My servant Moses; He is faithful in all My house. I speak with him face to face, Even plainly, and not in dark sayings;

Dark sayings or dark speeches in the King James Version come from the Hebrew word *chiydah*,[vii] which means "a puzzle, hence, a trick, conundrum, sententious maxim:—dark saying (sentence, speech), hard question, proverb, riddle." Knowing what the angels are talking about, therefore, requires a spiritual understanding and patience in untying the knot to reveal the message.

In April 2014, for example, the weather service was predicting that a super cell storm would converge over our region, producing major tornado activity. I had been quickened to all the pre-storm coverage so I had been praying over our region and had alerted many others to be praying as well. On April 4, 2014, during the night, a loud clap of thunder woke me out of a deep sleep. My eyes shot open and kneeing beside my bed was my angel. As I focused my eyes on him, I heard him say, "Close the window and batten down the hatch; it's coming," even though I never saw his mouth move. Let me just say this—the fact that God would send an angel to speak to me this way is truly His humor because I am completely challenged when it comes to riddles, word puns, or clichés, even though God's loves to use them. So, of course, I have to completely rely on the Lord for His leading regarding the interruption. I know; I know; it's the glory of God to conceal a matter and the glory of kings to search it out (smile).

Here is the interesting part. "Batten down the hatch" is a nautical cliché that means "prepare for stormy weather" or "prepare to meet an emergency or face great difficulty." Twenty-four days later on April 28, 2014, a deadly tornado made its way through portions of Winston County just 45 minutes south of our home. And even though our community was under a good many tornado warnings during that time we were spared and experienced no tornados. Please pray for Winston County as they are still rebuilding their lives and homes.

In a similar event occurring only three years prior, almost to the day, on April 23, 2011, I woke with a vision of a woman wearing a sun visor and I heard the words "sun visor." Instantly I understood this to be a word pun—sun visor = Son visor. Later that day I saw in a vision a watchtower with dark clouds in the sky. I heard the words "Watchman. Post. Run. Quick. He makes darkness His covering." I quickly began to intercede but for what I didn't know; however, when the Lord sends a word for you to man your post it is best for you to man your post!

The following morning on April 24, 2011, again I heard "He makes darkness His covering."

On April 25, 2011, I heard once more "He makes darkness His covering."

When the Lord is being repetitive, it is imperative to pay attention. So, in recognizing this repetitive scripture reference I had to investigate this warning.

Psalms 18: 11-19 says:

He made darkness His secret place; His canopy around Him was dark waters and thick clouds of the skies. From the brightness before Him, His thick clouds passed with hailstones and coals of fire. The Lord thundered from heaven, and the Most High uttered His voice, Hailstones and coals of fire. He sent out His arrows and scattered the foe, Lightnings in abundance, and He vanquished them. Then the channels of the sea were seen, the foundations of the world were uncovered. At Your rebuke, O Lord, at the blast of the breath of Your nostrils. He sent from above, He took me; He drew me out of many waters. He delivered me from my strong enemy, from those who hated me, for they were too strong for me. They confronted me in the day of my calamity, But the Lord was my support. He also brought me out into a broad place. He delivered me because He delighted in me.

I want to take a minute to show a few points of interested from verse 14 as it holds some significance. "He sent out His arrows and scattered the foe, Lightnings in abundance, and He vanquished them." David uses the word "arrows," and this Hebrew word is chets, which comes from another Hebrew word chatsats,[viii] that means "to chop into, pierce or sever; hence, to curtail, to distribute". He also uses the word "lightning," which is the Hebrew word baraq,[ix] meaning "a flashing sword:—bright, glitter, lightning". Now there is another word that grabs my prophetic antennas and it is the word "vanquished". In the King James Verse the word is "discomfited"; the Hebrew word is hamam,[x] and it means "to disturb, drive, destroy:—break, consume, crush, destroy, discomfit, trouble, vex." Now I ask that you to keep these in your mind as I move forward in sharing this event.

On the morning of April 26, 2011, I heard the words "We have arrived!" and I instantly felt a surge of angelic activity. Then I heard the word "covered." Honestly I didn't really have any idea at this time what the angels were referring to; however, I knew that whatever it was, I was covered. Throughout the day, however, weather reports were coming in that our area had a very high tornado rating for the following day, which meant the likelihood of a tornado hitting our area was very high.

Early in the wee hours of the morning, 2:30AM to be exact on April 27, 2011, my husband and I were awakened by thunder and strikes of lightning, the smell of pine, and sounds of objects hitting our home. Upon opening the French doors of our bedroom that overlooks our backyard, we could hear the swirling vortex of the tornado and quickly gathered our children and ran to our safe place.

As the tornado passed, we could see through the flashes of lightning that our property, excluding our home, and our community had suffered great damage. We stood in awe over what had just occurred while attempting to notify the emergency management system—911. As the attempts failed due to the system also being damaged by the tornado, I heard the Father say, "Manmade systems will fail but I will never fail! He who dwells in the secret place of the Most High shall abide under the shadow of the Almighty." I immediately recognized this as Psalms 91:1. Overwhelmed by the enormous love and grace handed to us by the Father, my heart cried out for even more of Him. I wanted to run even further into His shadow as the fierceness of the raging storm faced the pure humanness of our beings. I stood awe inspired as the frailty of life in the face of that strength can only be protected by the hand of God—He is our 911.

Five days later on May 1, 2011, I had a dream. In this dream I saw snow falling like cotton covering our entire community. As I stood taking in this amazing phenomena, I noticed the sky swirling. Out of the swirling sky came an angel who was very tall. If I had to guess I would say he stood about 150-200 feet. He wore glasses and was clothed in leaves. He was looking very closely at the land and all the inhabitants. I understood the snow to be for the refreshing of the land with purity and righteousness and the leaves were for healing.

I have heard many say in retrospect of inclement weather that God is bringing His judgment on the people. This is just not the case. There will be a Day of Judgment when God will sit and judge; however, this is not that day.

Let's look back at Psalm 18:14: "He sent out His arrows and scattered the foe, Lightnings in abundance, and He vanquished them." The word "foe" is simply another word for an adversary an enemy. We are not God's enemies; we are His children. He doesn't send out spears or swords against us. He does not seek to crush or destroy us. He does not seek to curtail or cut us off. The adversary does this and who is the adversary? It is Satan. Romans 16:20 says, "And the God of peace will crush Satan under your feet shortly."

There are times when the battle for our destinies are so intense that the effects are felt and even displayed in the atmosphere. You might recall the great signs and wonders displayed as God fought for the destinies of the children of Israel in the book of Exodus.

Hearing Demons

"For we do not wrestle against flesh and blood, but against principalities, against powers, against the rulers of the darkness of this age, against spiritual hosts of wickedness in the heavenly places."
(Ephesians 6:12)

      When you have your spiritual ears open, along with the pretty voices of the angels, you'll also hear the growling voices of demons. Unfortunately, however, not all demonic voices are growling. In fact, at times it can be difficult to distinguish which camp is talking to you as demons are very misleading and can mimic holy voices. Sometimes in these tricky situations the Holy Spirit will simply highlight the voice inflection and intonation as they can be dead giveaways as to who is speaking. Other times the message itself will alert you. For example, one morning I was getting ready for work when I heard a conversation behind me between two demons. They were trying to devise a scheme to entice me. I heard, "What about ____?" in one demonic voice followed by a different demonic voice that said, "No, she would never fall for that. Her heart belongs to Goooooood now," as if he were emphasizing in utter disdain the word "God." I found that quite funny and encouraging. I believe the Lord allowed me to hear this discussion because I had previously fallen prey to this particular sin over and over again. Over time, however, I had been diligent in resisting the enticements with the help of the Holy Spirit and the enemy finally got it—this sin would no longer have a hold on me (James 4:7). Praise the Lord!

I know some prophetic people who discount everything that demons say. Even though I would never suggest listening to demonic instruction, as they are only capable of telling the truth when commanded to do so in the name of Jesus—and this is utterly painful for them—I do ponder everything spoken to me before the Lord, even when the voice is obviously demonic, simply because demons were initially created to serve God and their purpose has not changed. Remember, they are fallen angels. I think I just heard your jaw hit the floor (smile). Let me explain while you're picking up your jaw.

There are many purposes for seeing in the Spirit, none of which include ignoring the dark side but rather revealing it and unmasking it to all counter attack. How would you ever be effective against the powers of darkness if you choose to ignore the fact that they are there? Unfortunately, many churches today take this stand and in doing so their members are unarmed against the wiles of the devil and are suffering needlessly. As I am typing this I am hearing, "But we pray and ask God to take care of it." Well, that is a statement from the devil. Here is why prayer will only get you so far—God already "took care of it" when He sent His Son. Jesus defeated everything—nailed it to the

cross. It's a done deal. His work is finished. By this He made everything subject to man and gave you the authority to push back darkness.
Ephesians 5:11 says, "And have no fellowship with the unfruitful works of darkness, but rather expose them." You cannot expose the workings of the devil if you choose to pretend they are not there. It is this same thinking that has allowed Satan to gain so much territory. When Jesus sent out the 12, He said in Matthew 10:7-8, "As you go preach, saying, The kingdom of heaven is at hand. Heal the sick, cleanse the lepers, raised the dead, cast out demons. Freely you have received. Freely give." Hmm...well I have attended many modern churches where I have heard the proclamation of "the Kingdom of heaven is at hand"; a few churches that venture out into healing the sick; one or two who testify to having raised the dead but I have yet to attend a church that is willing to cast out demons. Don't get me wrong I am sure they are out there— my point is that they are few and far between and not by any means mainstreamed. Yet this was the very commissioning to the church from Jesus and a large part of His ministry on earth.

Imagine with me, if you will, the U.S. Army positioning itself to fight foreign troops. But instead of fighting the opponent the Army simply stood still and stated its allegiance to the United States. Allegiance is great, and allegiance is honored, but if the soldiers don't draw their weapons and fight, they will be overtaken. In any battle, the most effective army has taken time to study its opponent. The soldiers have overheard the strategies of the enemy and reviewed previous battles. They are prepared to counter attack whatever the enemy may throw at them. The spiritual battlefield is no different. Prophets, Seers, and Intercessors are all on the front lines of this spiritual battlefield receiving direct intelligence and communication from heaven[xi].

What I have discovered is that it's really easy to move in the opposite spirit and counter attack when you listen to what is said to you. I give my eyes and ears to the Lord daily and command everything brought before me to be obedient to the Lord Jesus Christ. I daily renew my mind with scriptures and commit my thoughts to Him, taking every thought captive.

I understand that God is sovereign and nothing happens in my life without Him being aware of it and allowing it. So whatever the Father allows to be brought before my eyes and ears is for a purpose and I do not discount them but rather work with Him to counter attack all from a place of rest.

I do want to caution that I do not engage in "friendly" conversation with demons, however, for that would be foolish. Remember, Ephesians says, "have not fellowship with darkness," which means we are not to commune with demons. I am not talking about communion; I am talking about merely taking nothing for granted and taking every opportunity to turn a curse into a blessing.

Let me give you an example of listening and then counter attacking. This will empower those who are being tormented by demonic voices. I go into a lot of oppressed areas where demonic entities routinely try to linger around me. On this particular occasion, I heard one demon talking and he was really nasty. His words were just riddled with foul speech and curse words. Every time I rebuked him, he would leave briefly and then come right back. So finally I told the Father I was so tired of listening to this demon, and I thanked Him for giving me dominion and power over him. Then I declared and decreed that for every time I had to listen to this foul, nasty-speaking demon there will be 1,000 souls claimed for the kingdom of God in the name of Jesus Christ, according to Job 22:28, which says, "You will also declare a thing, and it will be established for you." The demon immediately let out a string of curse words, and I said, "Ok, that's a 1,000 souls I claim for God's kingdom in the name of Jesus." Then I heard the demon start to say something else and stopped short of completing his word. Ah, what a blessing it is to utilize the power I hold in Jesus Christ. If I had chosen to ignore the cursing, he would have never been silenced. In fact, he probably would have just stepped up his game if I hadn't stood against him or stopped the attack. Because I did not discount it, but rather chose to walk in the power of the Lord Jesus Christ over him, however, 1,000 souls were claimed for the Kingdom of God.

Hearing the Spirit of a Man

"For if I pray in a tongue, my spirit prays, but my understanding is unfruitful."

(1 Corinthians 14:14)

After a while, this gift of hearing in the Spirit advanced. When God gives you a small portion of a gift, and then you steward that gift, God will give you more, according to Luke 16:10. This is exactly what happened with hearing in the spirit. One day I was lying down, resting and worshiping the Lord, when suddenly I heard the voice of a friend of mine, who lives a couple of states away, praying in tongues. I jumped up and wrote down the phrase I heard and called her. She said, "Oh my goodness, Erica, I was just praying in tongues and that phrase is spoken very often but I don't know what it means." 1 Corinthians 14:14 tells us, "For if I pray in a tongue, my spirit prays, but my understanding is unfruitful." I was hearing her spirit praying and I suddenly remembered the question the Lord posed to me in a dream regarding the possibility of hearing the spirit of a man.

Several days later, I heard her voice again, only this time, it was being amplified through a microphone as if I were hearing her in a large stadium. This time I heard her say "The rhema word of God." I called her and she said God had given her a prophecy a few years back that she would be using her voice to speak His words. The Lord wanted to encourage her to hold onto this prophecy that was spoken over her.

Hearing the Thoughts and Intents of the Heart

"For the word of God is living and powerful, and sharper than any two-edged sword, piercing even to the division of soul and spirit, and of joints and marrow, and is a discerner of the thoughts and intents of the heart." (Hebrews 4:12)

"Samuel answered Saul and said, 'I am the seer. Go up before me to the high place, for you shall eat with me today; and tomorrow I will let you go and will tell you all that is in your heart.'"

(1 Samuel 9:19)

      Sometimes when I am worshiping the Lord, He allows me to hear the hearts of His people. Many times these hearts are distressed. It is no light thing to be entrusted with the hearts of men. I remember on one particular occasion I heard a man's voice that sounded as though he was speaking through a CB radio. He was distressed and crying out to the Lord. I knew the Lord allowed me to hear his heart because he needed someone to agree with him in prayer. So I did.

One morning as I was praying, in a vision, the Lord showed me the earth from an aerial viewpoint. Then I heard the Lord say, "Listen." As I did, I began to hear prayers from all around the world at the same time. It was as though I was standing in a packed stadium and heard everyone talking at once, and yet I could hear individual voices with specific prayers. Then the Lord changed the frequency, so to speak, and I heard the angels sing. There are simply no words in the English language to describe this sound.

Sometimes I will simply be going about my day when suddenly I will hear a friend's voice. He or she might say, "Erica knows" or "Ask Erica," or I might hear a more complex sentence. The most recent of these experiences I can think of right now occurred just a couple of weeks ago. I was getting ready for work when suddenly I heard my friend Kat's voice say, "Erica." I sent her a quick text telling her that I just heard her say my name.

She replied, "Well, it's because I was just thinking of you. I had a dream last night and the Lord told me you had the interpretation."

Section Four:
The Fight

The Battle with Fear

"For God has not given us a spirit of fear, but of power and of love and of a sound mind." (2 Timothy 1:7)

Up to this point, I have shared many of my "firsts" with regards to learning to use my Seer gift, as well as a few vitally important lessons I have learned along the way. Most of what I've shared was taken from years of flowing in this gifting. Equally important to learning and growing in my gifting, however, is learning how to stand my ground and contend for my right to walk in the high calling of Jesus Christ. The Lord said to me one day, "Erica, walking in the high calling comes at a price." I am reminded of these words found in Acts 9:16, "For I will show him how many things he must suffer for My name's sake."

So in light of this, I think it is imperative that I share with you the first and hardest battle I had to fight after receiving the Seer gift.

I am going to be completely transparent here and tell you that when the Lord first opened my eyes I was in awe of everything. I was stunned at the "now" reality of the word, the presence of angels, the existence of demons, and the overwhelming presence of the spiritual realm. The spiritual realm is an extremely active place and I was like a child on Christmas morning, wanting to share everything I saw with everyone I saw. I wanted to free everyone from the demons who lived in their homes and in their lives. I was excited beyond words at this new truth and gift the Lord had given me.

Unfortunately, when I shared everything I saw with everyone I saw, I discovered no one was interested. In fact, most everyone looked at me like I was crazy—literally! These were "church" people not some random strangers on the street—church people. People who were faithful to fill their spot on the church pew every Sunday. People who held offices such as teachers and deacons—church people. Soon after sharing my experiences I began to hear rumors of a few talking about "Erica seeing things and hearing voices." I soon realized I was Joseph, sharing my visions and dreams to a sect of believers who had not had their religious box of God destroyed. Without realizing it, I was asking them to perceive spiritual things when they were not spiritual, but religious. The reality of 1 Corinthians 2:14 hit me hard as I began to experience persecution on a level I had never known before: "But the natural man does not receive the things of the Spirit of God, for they are foolishness to him; nor can he know them, because they are spiritually discerned."

Sure, a few people enjoyed hearing about the occasional angel, but if I mentioned seeing a demon, all of a sudden expressions changed and it was as though I suddenly began speaking a different language. I remember thinking, *God...they are reading the same Bible I am, right?*

Absolutely astonished at reactions from "church people" and completely heartbroken, I retreated to God. "Father," I said, "how can this be? How can your people who claim to be Christians act in such a way? How can they choose to only 'believe' parts of your Word?"

After a brief pause, I heard Him say, "Erica, is it worth it?" I knew what He meant. He was asking me if I felt in my heart that He was worth the persecution I would face by walking in the Seer gift. I had to really think about the answer I would give Him because I understood what 2 Timothy 3:12 says about persecution: "Yes, and all who desire to live godly in Christ Jesus will suffer persecution." Then I remembered what the Lord said to Ananias regarding the Saul of Tarsus: "Go, for he is a chosen vessel of Mine to bear My name before Gentiles, kings, and the children of Israel. For I will show him how many things he must suffer for My name's sake."

I took some time to really ponder this question from the Lord. I began to think of all the experiences I had in His presence, and in a very short time I had come to understand the Lord in a way that only made me love Him more. I couldn't imagine a life without Him. So when I returned to the Lord with my answer, it was a resounding "Yes! Yes, you are worth it!"

You see, God is a gentleman. He invites you on a journey with Him but He is never going to force you to walk with Him. He invites you to drink of His cup but He will never force you to do so. He wants you to want Him as much as He wants you. He wants you to choose Him over the battle you'll have to endure to be with Him. I had to choose Him. I had to firmly place my foot on His path because the Lord knew the time would come when I would be sifted. The battle would be great and the struggle would be intense. I had to be resolved in my decision to completely commit to Him because my sanity would depend on it.

Make no mistake: the enemy hates you with an intensity that is unfathomable. He cares *nothing* about you and wants to utterly *destroy* you. He works very well under the cover of darkness, in the shadows of our minds, in the brokenness of our hearts, and in religious traditions and doctrines. So when you are seeing in the Spirit and begin to expose his works, he gets very defensive. Don't think for second that he is not going to retaliate. Don't think that he is not going to defend the turf he has gained. The retaliation he had planned for me ended up manifesting as a full frontal attack on my mind in the form of fear. This is one of the enemy's favorite ways to attack. If he can render you fearful, he has made you ineffective against him.

It was a beautiful fall day in 1999 when I suddenly became afraid. As odd as it sounds, I was suddenly and all at once fearful. I wasn't afraid of anything in particular but rather everything made me fearful. I suddenly became afraid to be alone, afraid to be in a crowd, afraid to drive down the highway, and afraid to stay home. I wasn't sleeping because I was afraid of what would happen if I went to sleep. Even worse, I was afraid to tell anyone that I was afraid. I couldn't even tell my husband. I felt like a prisoner locked inside a bubble of fear. I could remember the life I had just a couple weeks before where I wasn't afraid of anything. I literally felt my sanity slipping through my fingers and I was helpless to stop it, or so the enemy wanted me to think. After several weeks of this, I was emotionally, mentally, and physically exhausted.

One afternoon as I was pondering the upcoming drive I was about to have to make to pick up my kids in carpool, I was somewhat relieved to leave the house because I was so afraid to be there, but when I got in the car I was terrified to be there, as well. I remember thinking, *I have got to go get my children,* so I mustered the strength to pull out of my carport and make it to the end of my driveway. But that was as far as I got. Sitting there at the intersection of my driveway and the highway, I became frozen in fear. I couldn't go any farther. It was such an odd feeling. I was afraid to go back to the house, yet I was afraid to pull onto the road. I remember thinking, *This is it; I have truly lost my mind.* Then the fear escalated into full-on panic. It was the most terrified I had ever been, and it was literally because of nothing.

Totally disgusted by this feeling of constant fear, I was somehow able to whisper, "Jesus, help me."

As soon as I whispered those words I heard, "Erica, remember whose you are. You are mine and I did not give you a spirit of fear but of power, and love, and a sound mind. You have got to stand. Do not be afraid."

All at once I remembered some basic principles I had learned just a few weeks prior in Matthew 16:19: "and I will give you the keys of the kingdom of heaven, and whatever you bind on earth will be bound in heaven, and whatever you loose on earth will be loosed in heaven." Softly, at first, I began to simply praise Jesus for being my Savior and thanked Him for loving me. Then with power and amplitude in my voice, I began to bind the spirit of fear and loose the Holy Spirit to take over all areas it had tried to steal. Even louder and with more intensity I declared and decreed all areas of my life to be free from the spirit of fear in Jesus' name.

I immediately started feeling the grip of fear loosen, and within minutes it was completely gone. As quickly as it came, it left in Jesus' name. I felt as though a haze of darkness had lifted and I was able to see the Lord filtering the most beautiful rays of light through the trees. Being encouraged now, I pulled out of my driveway with confidence and courage.

Although I had won this battle, the war was not over. The memory of that struggle lingered in my heart and it became a tool of separation the enemy used to ultimately cause me to lay my gift down and walk away from the Lord for a season. I was in a place that I don't want anyone to ever be in—a place of choosing a life without the struggle to be near God.

I have heard religious people say, "If it's hard, it's not of God." Well, that is just not true because John 16:33 says, "in this life you will have trials and tribulations." Walking with God is never easy because the enemy is relentless; however, the reward of walking with God is worth every battle we can endure. I didn't realize that when the spirit of fear was attacking me. I only knew I didn't want to ever walk through a battle that great again in my life. So I thought the only way to avoid it was to walk away from the reason I was attacked to begin with. My faulty reasoning was that if I walked away from God, the enemy wouldn't bother me anymore. The problem was I didn't want to walk away. I had grown to love the Lord on a personal level beyond words, yet I didn't want to face a battle like that ever again—conflicted and torn, I turned away.

For seven years I tried to ignore everything that had to do with the Lord. But because His gifts and callings are without repentance (meaning He doesn't take them back), I still had visions and dreams; I just ignored them. I got so entangled with sin and the pleasures of life that I made one bad choice after another.

The Lord extended immeasurable grace to me and allowed me to wander like this for a season. At the end of this period in my life, however, I came face to face with an important decision that could change my life forever.

I will remember this night clearly for the rest of my life, as it profoundly changed my heart on the gifts and callings of the Lord. I had gotten up in the middle of the night to get a drink of water, and upon returning to my bed, I had a vision. I saw myself standing on the side of a road, watching a man dying. As I watched the life drain out of him, the color of his skin changed from pink to gray. I watched as his piercing eyes cried out for help. As I sat there in my bed, watching this vision, I felt powerless to help him. I heard the Lord say to me, "Pray for him."

Immediately, I asked the Lord, "Who am I to pray? Look at what I have been doing. My prayers won't save this man." Nonetheless, I was obedient to the Lord and I prayed, and in that moment, a great thing happened. I began to understand that my gift of seeing was not about me at all. And my walking in disobedience was not only affecting my life, but it was also affecting the lives of those the Lord has called me to help. A holy fear set in as I began to understand the cascading effects of disobedience.

With this vision, I turned my heart back to the Father and humbled myself to seek forgiveness and renunciation for all I had done over the last seven years—I had a lot to repent for.

Pondering the Return

"And He said to me, "My grace is sufficient for you, for My strength is made perfect in weakness." (2 Corinthians 12:9)

It was a cool fall afternoon and I was wrapped up in a blanket and sitting on our porch swing. Only days before I had humbled myself before the Lord and turned my heart back to Him. Yet, as I sat there swinging back and forth, I was now pondering God's choice in this vessel—in me! "Who am I, Lord, that you would grant me such a gift? After all you revealed to me through this amazing gift of sight, I walked away after the first hard battle. I am simply not worthy of this great gift. In addition to my utter failure to stand, Lord, I am no one that anyone would listen to. Most assuredly someone else could do a better job for you. Lord, I am not popular. I don't have fame or fortune. Lord, who am I?" I was heartbroken over all I had done and couldn't imagine ever being successful at using this gift for kingdom purposes.

As I continued to swing and pour out one pathetic heartbroken excuse after another, I closed my eyes and was instantly taken to a place of overwhelming peace. Stillness and quietness was all I heard, and my heart felt a tangible love that simply washed over me. I felt a peace like I had not felt in years. It was so nice to be back in His presence—In His loving arms.

The day turned into evening and I was worshipping the Lord in a time of prayer when Jesus appeared to me in a vision. Upon taking His outstretched hand, He immediately took me to the heavens. I saw a stunning gold throne, crested with diamonds. Even though Jesus didn't say so, I knew the throne was mine. I took my seat and my entire perspective changed as I remembered Ephesians 2:4-6, "But God, who is rich in mercy, because of His great love with which He loved us, even when we were dead in trespasses, made us alive together with Christ and raised us up together, and made us sit together in the heavenly places in Christ Jesus,"

I suddenly saw the matters of the earth from a heavenly perspective. As I sat taking in the heavens, Jesus got down on one knee, looked me in the eyes, and said, "Erica, I need you to believe that you are My beloved. I need you to view life from this perspective." He then took my hand and the scene changed. We were now standing in a courtyard with rolling hills of vibrant green grass in the background. Just beyond us in the near distance stood radiant buildings that seem to reflect light from within. There was a glow that saturated the atmosphere with a level of joy and love not felt on this earth. As I stood among this breathtaking scene I watched a young girl who looked to be about seven years old walk toward me with outstretched arms. I instantly knew her yet I had never seen her. My heart was overwhelmed.

This was my daughter—the baby I miscarried. She was stunningly beautiful with long straight light brown hair. She reminded me so much of our first daughter when she was that age. Overwhelmed with emotion I was speechless as Grace hugged me. I had named her Grace shortly after the miscarriage. I couldn't bear the thought of our baby not having a name. So one day as I was mourning the loss and wondering whether the baby was a girl or a boy. I asked the Father what should the baby's name be? Very gently I heard the softest voice say "Grace. Name her Grace. For My daughter, My Grace is sufficient for you." I now knew this baby was a girl and she now had a name—Grace. Naming her seemed to help my heart heal from the loss as it acknowledged her as a being created by the Father and created with a purpose, even though I knew her purpose would be served in Heaven. What I also knew was that there was another reason why the Lord allowed me to meet Grace. He was yet again telling me "My daughter, My grace is sufficient for you and My strength is made perfect in your weakness. My Grace will give you a different perspective." I turned and looked with tears falling down my face at Jesus. He smiled so warmly and said, "Erica, enjoy your life and reflect this atmosphere. Reflect Heaven." I began to understand that heaven doesn't get bothered when we stumble. They're not up there fretting over our past mistakes. They're not dwelling in the past bogged down by mounds of regret. On the contrary, they are cheering us on with an eternal hope and everlasting joy with the assurance that we can all be overcomers. They know everything that happens in our lives on this earth God will use for our good.

You see, when we are seated far above all the cares of this life, we can then and only then see things as they really are. Remember the grasshoppers' situation in Numbers 13 and 14? The Lord desired to give Canaan, a land flowing with milk and honey, to the children of Israel; however, there was snag in the plan to possess the land—the Israelites had to defeat the residents, who by the way were giants!

When we see through the perspective of our earthy view, we can be overcome instead of being the overcomers. The enemy will appear as giants and the struggle will appear too great. This was the place where I was when I walked away from the Lord. The enemy seemed like giants to me, and I literally felt like a grasshopper that could be crushed at any time. I don't want anyone to ever feel as though the struggle is too great. The struggle is just great enough because Jesus is more than enough. The Lord will never lead you to a land to possess without giving you the power to overcome the resident giants.

In order to possess the land of your time, you must not fear the inhabitants. John 16:33 says, "These things I have spoken to you, that in Me you may have peace. In the world you will have tribulation; but be of good cheer; I have overcome the world."

"Enjoy my life, Jesus, what is my life? What is my purpose here? I don't know how to get people to listen to me. I am a nobody here."

Jesus softened His eyes and it felt as though rivers of compassion were released through His gaze as He said so softly, "The ones who will listen, will listen because they have a heart for Me. If their hearts are already hardened they haven't listened to Me and they won't listen to you. But, My child, that is not for you to worry about. Your burden is not to determine who will receive the truth but to carry it. Seeing truth is a choice." As He continued I felt as a small child sitting on her father's lap yet I really had no idea what that felt like. My father died when I was a baby. So I never knew the love of a father, however, in this moment I felt completely transparent and nothing was hidden from my Father's eyes. Years of loneliness seemed to surface as I heard the following words:

"I Am your Father and I have always been here for you. There were times in your life when you have felt so alone. In fact, most of your life you have felt this way. Isolated. My beloved, I have not isolated you, however, I have set you apart from the beginning. I chose you before you knew Me. I caused you to not fit in. For My purposes you needed not be a part of the world. You needed to not have any identity with this world—no kinship. Your eyes and heart needed to be on Me—your kinship is in Me. So many times you tried so hard to fit in with the world and it only
brought destruction. You were at war with yourself because that was not your calling—not your

destiny. My beloved, you must set your eyes on Me."

With these piercing words the vision faded and I was left back in my room, but for the first time in my life I felt as though I truly had a purpose in this life. Suddenly all of my years of wondering seemed to make sense now and I was able to be at peace with all I had endured throughout my life.

Blessed Vengeance

"God is jealous, and the Lord avenges; The Lord avenges and is furious. The Lord will take vengeance on His adversaries, And he reserves wrath for His enemies;"

(Nahum 1:2)

After the matter of perspective and calling was settled in my heart and in my mind, the Lord said to me that the very thing the enemy used to lure me away He would turn for my good. It would become a strength and not a weakness, and He would use it to snatch others from the fire of the enemy. This is the vengeance of the Lord.

I was restored with love, a peace that passes all understanding, and an unwavering faith. I would no longer become shaken when I come face to face with a demon and the battle he brings. In fact, during the final stages of writing this book, one morning I came face to face with a demonic entity that literally stood nose to nose with me. The intensity of the evil and hatred that was emanating from this being was on a level I had never experienced before. This told me that with the publication of this book I would be entering into a new land—and there would be new giants to overcome. This time, however, I didn't feel like a grasshopper looking up at a giant. Instead, I stood face to face with him and I stood unshaken. I now understand how to operate within the Seer gift without fear and without torment. I can walk into this land because I do not walk alone. I have a promise from the Lord that He will never leave me nor forsake me. I have learned the power of the blood of Jesus and the sovereign authority that resides in His name. Because of this, I can view the enemy and not be overcome because I am viewing him from a place that is hidden under the wings of the Almighty—I am hidden in Christ!

Soon after my return to the Lord, I visited Apostle Dennis Arnold's church in South Alabama where I received a powerful confirmation. Apostle Arnold prophesied over me, saying, "Erica, God has given you a peace that passes all understanding because you will encounter on the road ahead times not filled with peace. For you have been created for the end time's battle."

God gives us a peace that the world seeks. This kind of peace is only found in Jesus Christ. We can't produce it in a pill and we can't replicate it in witchcraft. We can only find it by seeking first His Kingdom and His righteousness and utterly delighting ourselves in Him. For 1 John 4:17-19 says:

> Love has been perfected among us in this: that we may have boldness in the day of judgment; because as He is, so are we in this world. There is no fear in love; but perfect love casts out fear, because fear involves torment. But he who fears has not been

made perfect in love. We love Him because He first loved us.

Contact Information:

erica-christopher@usa.net

Website:

www.ericachristopher.com

End Notes

[i] Bob Larson. Larson's Book of World Religions and Alternative Spirituality. Wheaton, IL: Tyndale House, 2004. 524-26. Print.

[ii] James Strong. A Concise Dictionary of the Words In The Hebrew Bible; With Their Renderings In The Authorized English Version. Madison, NJ, 1890. Print. Strong's Hebrew Dictionary 1304. בָּרֶקֶת bareqeth. Search for H1304 in KJVSL. בָּרֶקֶת bareqeth baw-reh'-keth or barkath {baw-rek-ath'}; from 1300; a gem (as flashing), perhaps the emerald—carbuncle. See Hebrew 1300.

[iii] James Strong. A Concise Dictionary of the Words In The Hebrew Bible; With Their Renderings In The Authorized English Version. Madison, NJ, 1890. Print. Strong's Hebrew Dictionary 4805. מְרִי m@riy. Search for H4805 in KJVSL. מְרִי mriy mer-ee'. Taken from Strong's Hebrew Dictionary 4784. מָרָה marah. Search for H4784 in KJVSL מָרָה marah maw-raw' a primitive root; to be (causatively, make) bitter (or unpleasant); (figuratively) to rebel (or resist; causatively, to provoke)—bitter, change, be disobedient, disobey, grievously, provocation, provoke(-ing), (be) rebel (against, -lious).

[iv] James Strong. A Concise Dictionary of the Words In The Hebrew Bible; With Their Renderings In The Authorized English Version. Madison, NJ, 1890. Print. Strong's Hebrew Dictionary 1304. בָּרֶקֶת bareqeth. Search for H1304 in KJVSL. בָּרֶקֶת bareqeth baw-reh'-keth or barkath {baw-rek-ath'}; from 1300; a gem (as flashing), perhaps the emerald—carbuncle. See Hebrew 1300.

[v] James Strong. A Concise Dictionary of the Words In The Hebrew Bible; With Their Renderings In The Authorized English Version. Madison, NJ, 1890. Print. Strong's Hebrew Dictionary 1300. בָּרָק bara. Search for H1300 in KJVSL. בָּרָק baraq baw-rawk' from 1299; lightning; by analogy, a gleam. concretely, a flashing sword—bright, glitter(-ing sword), lightning. See Hebrew 1299.

[vi] James Strong. A Concise Dictionary of the Word in The Greek New Testament; With Their Renderings in the Authorized English Version. Madison, NJ. Strong's Greek Dictionary 1271. διανοια dianoia Search for G1271 in KJVSL διανοια dianoia dee-an'-oy-ah from 1223 and 3563; deep thought, properly, the faculty (mind or its disposition), by implication, its exercise:— imagination, mind, understanding. See Greek 1223. See Greek 3563.

[vii] James Strong. A Concise Dictionary of the Words In The Hebrew Bible; With Their Renderings In The Authorized English Version. Madison, NJ, 1890. Print. Strong's Hebrew Dictionary. 2420. חִידָה chiydah. Search for H2420 in KJVSL חִידָה chiydah khee-daw' from 2330; a puzzle, hence, a trick, conundrum, sententious maxim:—dark saying (sentence, speech), hard question, proverb, riddle.

[viii] James Strong. A Concise Dictionary of the Words In The Hebrew Bible; With Their Renderings In The Authorized English Version. Madison, NJ, 1890. Print. Strong's Hebrew Dictionary 2686. חָצַץ chatsats Search for H2686 in KJVSL חָצַץ chatsats khaw-tsats' a primitive root (compare 2673); properly, to chop into, pierce or sever; hence, to curtail, to distribute (into ranks); as denom. from 2671, to shoot an arrow:—archer, X bands, cut off in the midst. See Hebrew 2673. See Hebrew 2671

[ix] James Strong. A Concise Dictionary of the Words In The Hebrew Bible; With Their Renderings In The Authorized English Version. Madison, NJ, 1890. Print. Strong's Hebrew Dictionary 1300. בָּרָק baraq Search for H1300 in KJVSL בָּרָק baraq baw-rawk' from 1299; lightning; by analogy, a gleam; concretely, a flashing sword:—bright, glitter(-ing sword), lightning. See Hebrew 1299

[x] James Strong. A Concise Dictionary of the Words In The Hebrew Bible; With Their Renderings In The Authorized English Version. Madison, NJ, 1890. Print. Strong's Hebrew Dictionary 2000. הָמַם hamam Search for H2000 in KJVSL הָמַם hamam haw-mam' a primitive root (compare 1949, 1993); properly, to put in commotion; by implication, to disturb, drive, destroy:—break, consume, crush, destroy, discomfit, trouble, vex.
See Hebrew 1949. See Hebrew 1993

[xi] Alec, Wendy. Visions from Heaven: Visitations to My Father's Chamber. Dublin, Ireland: Warboys, 2013. 117. Print.

Made in the USA
Columbia, SC
28 June 2020